THE AMERICAN CAUSE

OTHER BOOKS BY RUSSELL KIRK

Academic Freedom

Beyond the Dreams of Avarice

The Conservative Mind

A Program for Conservatives

Prospects for Conservatives [A Gateway edition]

The
American Cause

RUSSELL KIRK

HENRY REGNERY COMPANY

CHICAGO, 1957

Third Printing 1965

Table of Contents

v

Western politics · Meaning of justice · Meaning of order · Meaning of freedom · American polity · Contrast with French Revolution · "To each his own" · American concept of equality · Order and classless society · Meaning of aristocracy · Specific nature of American liberties · Unrestrained liberty · American political equilibrium

Source of authority · Pure democracy · Meaning of federalism · Limited government · Territorial democracy · State governments · Representatives · Federal government · Legislative power · Executive power · Judicial power · Vigor of American political system · Political parties · American government and sound security

Reasons for American belief in free enterprise · Danger of exaggerated economic slogans · Economic production a means to ends · Marx and "capitalism" · Meaning of Communism · Adam Smith · Definition of capital · Idea of competition · Motives to integrity · Compulsion as a substitute · Charity and competition · Servile economy · Social justice, true and false · Pure equality impossible · Totalist economy and disorder

American standard of living · Concentration of wealth · Millions of "capitalists" · American material achievements · American economic experience refutes Marx · Technology and freedom · Free enterprise and leisure · No depressed classes · Prosperity no guarantee of happiness · Misrepresentations of Communists · American economy vii

THE AMERICAN CAUSE

CHAPTER 1

Betrayal through Ignorance

Dangerous luxury

This little book is a statement of the moral and social principles which the American nation upholds in our time of troubles. It is not a collection of slogans, nor yet a history of American politics. Intended to be an honest description of the beliefs we Americans live by, *The American Cause* is a brief effort to refresh Americans' minds.

Many Americans are badly prepared for their task of defending their own convictions and interests and institutions against the grim threat of collectivism. The propaganda of Communists and other ideologues sometimes confuses and weakens the will of well-intentioned Americans who lack any clear understanding of their own nation's first principles. And in our age, when all civilization is immediately menaced by the designs of the Soviets, good-natured ignorance is a luxury none of us can afford.

American troops captured in Korea

Here is one illustration of our present confusion. The Chinese Communists, who took prisoner thousands of our soldiers in Korea, found to their high satisfaction that American troops were easy subjects for Communist indoctrination, because most American soldiers were ignorant of the principles and rights and political forms they were supposed to defend in the Korean War. In July, 1951, the Chief of Intelligence of the "Chinese People's Volunteer Army" in North Korea wrote a memorandum for his superior in Peiping: "An Estimate of American Military Personnel." Even after we have allowed for the exaggeration and hostility of this report, it remains an exposure of our weakness which we would ignore at our own peril. As an American officer comments, "No realistic person dismisses it as being entirely a figment of Communist imagination." Consider the following extract from this "Estimate":

Based upon our observations of American soldiers and their officers captured in this war for the liberation of Korea from capitalistic and imperialistic aggression, the following facts are evidenced. The American soldier has weak loyalties to his family, his community, his country, his religion, and his fellow soldiers. His concepts of right and wrong are hazy; opportunism is easy. By himself, he feels frightened and insecure. He underestimates his own worth, his own strength, and his ability to survive. He is largely ignorant of social values, social tensions and conflicts. There is little knowledge or understanding, even among United States university graduates, of American political history and philosophy; of the federal, state, and community organizations; of state rights and civil rights; of safeguards to freedom; and of how these things supposedly operate within his own system. He is exceedingly insular and provincial, with little or no idea of the problems and the aims of what he contemptuously describes as foreigners and their countries. . . . Based upon these facts about the imperialistic United States aggressors, the re-education and indoctrination program for American prisoners proceeds as planned.

This hostile assessment of American soldiers' convictions was confirmed, in substance, by the investigations which our own armed forces subsequently conducted into the conduct and morale of our troops that had been released from the Communist prisoner-of-war camps. As one American officer writes, "This is a commentary on manners and morals; on character and lack of it; on a disease that might well be considered the Number One Social Disease of America. Its prevention and its treatment are essential to the continuing survival of our system."

Most of the records of our captured troops are open to the inspection of any person seriously interested. The Air Force's documents on its personnel who were captured, which are particularly interesting, are available at Maxwell Field, Alabama, and at Harvard University. The Army has published a revealing booklet, "Communist Interrogation, Indoctrination, and Exploitation of Prisoners of War." Several officers and men have published their memoirs of prison-camp life. All these confirm the Communist Chief of Intelligence in his contemptuous observation that the American military man was ignorant of his own cause. And a sub-committee of the Senate concluded that the failure of our educational system to provide proper instruction in history, politics, economics, and other subjects was a principal cause of the bewildered and shameful conduct of the majority of American prisoners. We use the word "majority" deliberately: for it is the finding of our own armed services that *most* American soldiers succumbed in varying degrees without serious resistance.

Communist brainwashing

It rarely was torture or drugs that rendered our troops easy victims to the Communists; the records show that Communist "brainwashing" was simply clever political indoctrination, usually without physical intimidation. Our men were betrayed by their own ignorance, lack of confidence, and weakness in reasoned debate. Even the minority of prisoners—less than ten per cent of the total—who actively resisted such indoctrination scarcely could tell how or why they resisted, although they took to themselves, with pride, the epithet the Communists hurled at them, "Recreationaries." Among these "Reactionaries," formal schooling was not the only support for their resistance, it appears, nor even the primary one. Yet those "Reactionaries" who were better informed sometimes were better able to resist Communist indoctrination—and often with less physical hardship. It was not that they used their knowledge to argue with the enemy, so much as it was that their knowledge tended to reassure and fortify their minds. Their knowledge shored up their faith and loyalty; they were not left dependent simply on prejudice and stubbornness.

Something was wrong with our army in Korea; and something, it seems probable, was wrong with a nation that sent out such an army. A part of the trouble, which goes deep, is beyond the limits of this book. Yet a part of the trouble, obviously enough, is that our soldiers, and our people in general, do not understand clearly what they are fighting for, in our present struggle against the Communist power. This book cannot make up for the deficiencies in our system of schooling which have permitted such ignorance to prevail. All such a book as *The American Cause* can do is to outline, in a general way, the chief principles which are our nation's; and to stimulate, possibly, some interest in further study of these matters. For those who may wish to look into the subject, we have appended a brief list of other books on religious and moral principles, history, economics, and politics.

The meaning of ideology

Our book is intended for the general reader, civilian and military. We try not to take sides concerning religious and political questions which still are in dispute in America, but endeavor to state as simply as we can those great convictions upon which nearly all Americans seem to be agreed: to which most Americans agree, by their daily acceptance of these principles as rules of life and politics, even if they themselves cannot easily put their convictions into words. This book does not provide an American "ideology." The word ideology means political fanaticism, a body of beliefs alleged to point the way to a perfect society. Most Americans, this author included, are not political fanatics. But this book does provide, we trust, a concise statement of the beliefs which secure our order, our justice, and our freedom.

When, in the Second World War, our troops landed in North Africa, the French were astonished at how politically naïve American soldiers seemed. For most Frenchmen are passionately interested in political notions; while most Americans—like most English people—are not. This lack of interest in abstract politics is not necessarily always a harmful thing. One reason why the Americans, like the English, do not spend much time arguing over theories of politics is that for a very great while nearly all of us have been contented with our society and our form of government. We have not been revolutionaries since 1776, because we have felt that we have enjoyed as good a society as any people reasonably can hope for.

But nowadays, if we mean to defend against our totalitarian enemies all the good things in our society, we need to study and to think. We are terribly threatened by relentless opponents, the Communists, with the power of Soviet Russia behind them. We do not need to invent some new theory of human nature and politics; but we do need, urgently, to recall to our minds the sound convictions which have sustained our civilization and our nation. The totalitarian revolutionaries, no matter how powerful Russia may be, cannot defeat us if we are strong in our own principles. But if we seem to the rest of the world to stand for nothing; and if we ourselves are ignorant of those ideas and institutions which nurture our culture and our political liberty—why, then we will fall, no matter how great our industrial productivity is, and no matter how many divisions we equip, and no matter what ingenious new weapons we devise.

The Communist and the Nazi and the Fascist have drawn their strength from faith in their ideas, evil though most of their ideas have been. When a Chinese peasant conscripted to fight in Korea has more faith in his ideology than we have in our ancient principles, and when a hastily-drilled Communist indoctrinator can bewilder and subdue even American university graduates by his arguments, then our American cause is in great peril.

Our military authorities instructed our soldiers in Korea that, if they should be captured, they were not to argue political or economic questions with their Communist guards and interrogators; the odds seemed to be that our men would lose such arguments, and become correspondingly confused and dejected. If our troops, or even a reasonable proportion of them, had been at all prepared to resist the arguments of the Communists, and possibly to answer them, our record in Korea might have been very different. In the prison camps, our men died by the thousands—not from physical mistreatment, except in a few instances, but principally from despair, bewilderment, and lack of faith. It ought to have been otherwise. And in the battle lines, and behind the lines, some general understanding of the American cause would have helped our army, and our nation, immeasurably.

Of the thousands of American soldiers and civilians

captured by the Communists in Asia, very few emerged from prison unbroken in spirit and undefeated, morally and intellectually, by the enemy. One of those few who triumphed over adversity was a Catholic priest, Father Harold W. Rigney. Now Father Rigney knew how to argue, and he argued with his jailers; he knew what his religion and his civilization and his nation stood for, and he defended those principles; he surprised and discouraged his Communist interrogators. It is improbable that he convinced or converted his jailers, but surely he embarrassed them, and in time they quietly "expelled" him from China, rather than have so disturbing a prisoner in touch with the local populace and their own agents and officials. Such a man is hard to beat. Yet it is not only priests or especially-schooled people who can beat the Communists: any intelligent American who knows his own principles can do that work. Some American soldiers in Korea similarly disturbed the Communists—but too few.

Now most of the American prisoners who succumbed to the process of indoctrination called "brainwashing" did not actively embrace Communism. Nor did the Chinese Communists expect them to do so.* All that the

---

* The term "brainwashing" has been widely employed in American newspapers and books to mean simply systematic indoctrination in Communist ideology. Strictly speaking, however, the Chinese device of "brainwashing" is a most elaborate and lengthy process, intended to uproot altogether the subject's previous convictions and to convert him wholeheartedly to Communism. In this stricter sense only a few American prisoners, military or civilian, were subjected to real brainwashing. Father Rigney,

Communists hoped to achieve—and in this they succeeded—was to diminish the faith of the Americans in their own country, their cause, and their fellow-soldiers and fellow-citizens. Most of the Americans did not become Communists; but they ceased to be actively hostile toward Communism, and they ceased to struggle in any way, even by passive resistance, against their captors. They became apathetic and submissive; they caused little trouble for their jailers. As one former prisoner in Korea has put it, "In their efforts to dominate the minds of men, the Communists do not insist on actual acceptance of their ideology, only submission to it. Communist ideological conquests depend not primarily on the strength of the Communist ideology, but on the weakness of the opposition."

Communism and ignorance

For the present, the Korean war is over. Those of our soldiers who survived their loneliness and despair are free again. But the Communist challenge presumably will be confronting Americans for a long while to come; and it is doubtful whether, in another hour of trial, our troops would be found better prepared to resist the falsi-

---

who was of this smaller number, resisted with complete success. The great majority of American prisoners were not truly "brainwashed," but only compelled to attend indoctrination classes and persuaded to cooperate in Communist propaganda-devices. The object of the Communist indoctrinators, in this great majority of cases, seems to have been to confuse and dishearten the prisoners by weakening their old loyalties, rather than to make enduring conversions to Communism.

fications and insinuations of the Communists. It is doubtful whether the great majority of American citizens are possessed of any clear understanding of those differences of principle which distinguish their society from that of their adversaries. And this is a perilous condition. There is small danger that the majority of Americans ever will embrace Communism actively. But there is considerable danger that the majority of Americans may fail, like our prisoners of war, to oppose Communism intelligently. Communists do not require, or even desire, that Communist doctrines be accepted with enthusiasm. What Communism flourishes upon is the indifference and the ignorance of the majority.

We need badly some millions more of Americans who are hard to beat. Our immediate task, it seems, is to reaffirm the faith that has been our nation's. Nowadays we Americans—as Edmund Burke said of Englishmen in the time of the French Revolution—"are combatting an armed doctrine." That armed and fierce doctrine against which we fight just now is Communism. Not long ago, it was Naziism; in the future, it may be some fresh fanatic challenge to the things we love. Our American principles, we think, will stand the test of such a ferocious assault—if only we know those principles. A fanatic armed doctrine can be resisted only by a strong body of sound principles.

Demosthenes, the great Athenian patriot, cried out to his countrymen when they seemed too confused and divided to stand against the tyranny of Macedonia: "In God's name, I beg of you to think." For a long while, most Athenians ridiculed Demosthenes' entreaty: Macedonia was a great way distant, and there was plenty of time. Only at the eleventh hour did the Athenians perceive the truth of his exhortations. And that eleventh hour was too late. So it may be with Americans today. If we are too indolent to think, we had might as well surrender to the totalitarians tomorrow. This small book, despite all its limitations, possibly may encourage some thought.

CHAPTER 2

The Need for Principles

The American cast of mind

Most Americans do not wish to turn the world upside down. By and large, the American people have shown a conservative cast of mind ever since they achieved their independence. Struggle among classes rarely has been fierce in the United States; Americans have been content with their domestic pattern of life and politics. And, except for a few brief interludes, we have intervened in the affairs of other states only reluctantly; we have built no great American empire, and have not attempted to impose American patterns of life and forms of government upon the rest of the world.

For a great power—today the greatest of the powers—the United States has been an astonishingly tranquil and unbelligerent nation. We have known only one violent internal conflict, the Civil War, and that nearly a century ago. We have prospered exceedingly in a material way. We have maintained a degree of order and justice and freedom very rare in history. And behind these outward marks of success lie certain enduring principles of thought and action which, in very considerable part, have created and protected our national life. Certain concepts in men's minds are responsible for our private rights, our sound government, and our worldly prosperity.

Though most men and women, in any age and any country, live almost unaware that they are governed by certain general ideas, nevertheless nearly everything we have is produced and sheltered by the moral and intellectual assumptions that people take for granted. One cannot see or feel or taste or hear ideas; yet without the existence of great ideas, human beings would be only animals, and could exist only as animals live. Only mankind possesses ideas. The success or failure of any human society depends upon how sound and true its ideas are. That a nation has prospered a great while—that it has been orderly and free and just and wealthy—is one very good proof that its ideas have been sound and true.

Three bodies of principle controlling any people

Three groups of ideas, or bodies of principle, invisibly control any people, whether those people are Australian bushmen or highly civilized modern nations. The first, and most important, of these bodies of principle is the set of moral convictions which a people hold: their ideas about the relationship between God and man, about virtue and vice, honesty and dishonesty, honor and dishonor. The second of these bodies of principle is the set of political convictions which a people hold: their ideas about justice and injustice, freedom and tyranny, personal rights and power, and the whole complex problem

13

of living together peaceably. The third of these bodies of principle is the set of economic convictions which a people hold: their ideas about wealth and property, public and private responsibilities in the affair of making a living, and the distribution of goods and services.

Out of the development of these bodies of principle there grows what we call civilization; and when these bodies of principle are weakened, and a people lose faith in the ideas by which they live, civilization decays. When these bodies of principle are increasing in strength and richness, we say a people are progressive; but when these bodies of principle are decaying in their influence upon men and women, we call such a people decadent. It is by the healthiness of our principles that we measure the success or failure of any society.

These bodies of principle have come into existence among us by a long and mysterious process. Only man recognizes principles, and only man knows civilization. These principles have been built up over a great many centuries, most of them: they are the accumulated accomplishment of countless generations of human beings. We do not know how or when most of them first were recognized by men. Occasionally, in the procession of history, a man of genius contributes something new to these principles, or revives and improves some principle long neglected. But for the most part these ideas are the product of innumerable thinking and working men and women, who come to agree that a particular concept is true. By an age-long process of trial and error—straining men's notions through the sieve of history—some human beliefs are found to be sound and enduring, while others are found to be erroneous and obsolete. Yet a number of human convictions have persisted ever since civilization began, little changed by the passage of time; these seem to be permanent truths, which any civilized nation must reckon with or else decay.

Most Americans are convinced that certain of these enduring truths were revealed to mankind by God: among these principles are the necessity for worshipping the Creator, the essence of private morality, and the nature of love which teaches us our duties toward other men and women. The powers and the limits of human nature, Americans have felt, have been implanted in our minds by divine revelation.

But the majority of the principles by which we live, Americans generally seem to agree, are the product of human experience through the ages, as man struggled up from savagery toward civilization: now making progress, now slipping into decadence. Our convictions about the administration of justice, for instance, and the better patterns of government, and the proper functioning of the economy, are derived from the "wisdom of the species," the trial-and-error lessons of history—though, it should be added, even our system of justice, our forms of law and order, and our economic ways seem to most Americans to be our imperfect human attempts to reproduce in society certain natural laws for human conduct which a divine intelligence decreed.

Origin of our moral, political, and economic ideas

Now these general principles to which most Americans are attached are not themselves—with a very few exceptions—of purely American origin. Our religious and moral convictions had their origin in the experience and thought of the ancient Jews and Greeks and Romans. Our political ideas, for the greater part, are derived from Greek and Roman and medieval European and especially English practice and philosophy. Our economic concepts, some of them, can be traced back to the age of Aristotle and beyond; and even the more recent of these economic ideas were first expressed in eighteenth-century Britain and France, rather than in America. American civilization does not stand by itself: it is part of a great chain of culture which we sometimes call "Western civilization," or "Christian civilization," yet which in some particulars is older even than the culture of Western Europe or the history of Christianity.

Americans, nevertheless, have adapted these ancient principles to the circumstances of life in their country, and often have improved the practical application of these ideas to the workaday world. The Americans, like the Romans, have been conspicuously a people of practical talents. Sometimes they have been so much occupied with practical matters that they have almost forgotten how everything practical really is the application of a general principle. Yet even our immense industrial and technological achievements are possible only through the application of certain scientific theories to achieve material results. The more civilized people become, the more do they depend upon general ideas. Only the primitive savage manages to get along, after a fashion, in a "practical" way, without much reference to moral and intellectual concepts. (But even the savage recognizes and obeys some general ideas, if expressed only as taboos and ancient customs.) The savage remains a savage if he does not acquire general principles about which to form his life. The civilized man sinks back into savagery when he forgets the principles which have made possible his material accomplishments.

We cannot understand our American cause, therefore, unless we first understand the principles upon which the American people have formed their complex society. In the chapters which follow, we shall look at the moral convictions of Americans, and see how these moral convictions have been expressed in our national life. We shall look at the political convictions of Americans, and see how these political convictions have shaped the American government. We shall look at the economic convictions of Americans, and see how these economic convictions have accounted for the growth of American industry and commerce. These chapters, in short, will combine a description of Americans' opinions with a brief account of American institutions. The American cause, the purpose and duty and mission of the United States in the twentieth-century world, has grown out of these bodies of principle and out of the practical American experience in the application of these principles. The American, as a type, is not a visionary, a dreamer: he acts upon long-established principles which have been confirmed as valid by the American historical experience. And the American cause is not some vague aspiration toward turning the world upside down, but a sober and prudent defense of beliefs and rights and institutions—the legacy of civilization—which today are threatened by violent and disastrous forces that would kill our culture.

Principles and civilization

A man without principles is an unprincipled man. A nation without principles is an uncivilized nation. If a people forget their principles, they relapse into barbarism and savagery. If a people reject sound principles for false principles, they become a nation of fanatics. The thinking American nowadays has to defend sound principle on two fronts: one, the neglect of all principle which leads to social and personal decadence; the other, the adoption of false principles which plunges the world into anarchy. Our danger at home is that a great part of the American people may forget that enduring principles exist. Our danger abroad is that the false principles of revolutionary fanaticism, at present represented by international Communism, may gain such an influence as to wound us terribly. The American cause, then, is the defense of the principles of a true civilization. This defense is conducted by renewing men's consciousness of true moral and political and economic principle, and by applying true principle to the institutions of society and private life.

The Need for Principles

Americanism and American belief

So this book is not written to convert Americans into political fanatics, zealous for a vague "Americanism" to be extended over the whole world. Nor is this book written as a piece of propaganda to persuade other peoples that everything American is perfect. One of the most important and beneficial aspects of our American tradition, indeed, is toleration: and this toleration extends to a sympathetic approval of variety, national and private rights, and freedom of choice, both at home and throughout the world. The American mission is not to make all the world one America, but rather to maintain America as a fortress of principle and in some respects an example to other nations. The American cause is not to stamp out of existence all rivals, but simply to keep alive the principles and institutions which have made the American nation great.

We propose, in this book, to steer clear of "devil terms" and "god terms." We shall not argue that a thing is good simply because it is American, or bad simply because it is not American; our endeavor will be to describe the essence of American belief and practice, without preaching a crusade for Americanism. We shall try to remain free of slogans and clichés. We are not going to oppose an abstract "capitalism" to an abstract "communism," or an abstract "democracy" to an abstract "absolutism" or "imperialism." Thinking in slogans ends with thinking in bullets. When we speak of democracy, we shall speak of democratic institutions in the United States, not of some misty political ideal that Americans are expected to impose on the universe. When we speak of economic free enterprise, we shall speak of economic practices and developments in the United States, not of some Utopia of perfect competition. In much of the world, political discussion has degenerated into a Babel of furious voices, all crying out abstract god-terms and devil-terms that bear small relation to real governments, or real economies, or real men and women. The American cause cannot be explained or served by strident propaganda of that sort. And the American cause is so complex and living a thing, grown out of such an ancient soil, that it cannot be described in single phrases like "capitalism" or "democracy" or "equality." On the contrary, the American cause is made up of many moral and political and economic factors, some of them peculiar to America.

Confused foreign impressions of America

No cause can be maintained long unless a considerable proportion of a people understand the meaning of that cause. It seems to us that the number of people who truly understand the complexity of the American cause has grown dangerously small. The bewilderment and weakness of our troops in Korea was only one small symptom, though a striking one, of how many Americans have ceased to understand either the principles or the institutions which make up American civilization. There are many other such symptoms. Some of our official representatives abroad, and many of our travellers, are unable to explain American things to Europeans and

Asiatics and Africans: sometimes they apologize confusedly for things that need no apology, or belligerently assert that all things American necessarily are better than all things foreign, and that "American know-how" might solve all the problems of humanity. Within the United States, a dismayingly large number of people seem to assume that our order and justice and freedom and prosperity will continue forever, with no need of *their* help; if they think at all about the forces which keep American society vital, they seem to think of the nation's life as a kind of machine, tended by someone in Washington, from which they have an absolute right to benefit but to which they are obliged to contribute nothing.

And among other people, the impression has been gaining strength—encouraged by the deliberate agitation of political fanatics—that America is a prosperous barbarian nation, swaggering and covetous, engaged in some design to extend its power over the universe. Or, in a different vein, some men and women in other countries think dreamily of the United States as a place of unbounded resources and endless amusements—and are envious accordingly. There is need for reminding the rest of the world that America is not merely an abstraction, a work of nature: for America really is a highly civilized nation whose achievement has been made possible by the union of enduring traditions with private energies and public responsibilities.

This book is a little window opening on the beliefs and customs and history and practices in America which con-

21

stitute America's claim to civilization and America's source of well-being. We have written it as a work of renewal, of restoration, in a modest way: a reminder that "the dead alone give us energy," that today's policy must be undertaken in the light of yesterday's experience, and that the American cause has become the cause of all high culture.

CHAPTER 3

Moral Principle: The Nature of Man

The United States a Christian nation

The United States is a Christian nation. This is a simple statement of fact, not an argument to advance the American cause. With the exception of the five and a half million American Jews, professed Christians or people strongly influenced by Christianity make up almost the whole of our population. Christianity and Judaism, moreover, come from a common origin, share many centuries of common historical experience, and have in part the same body of literature, those books of the Bible which Christians call the Old Testament; and so far as what can be said in this little book about moral and religious principle is concerned, the differences between Christian and Jewish belief are minor. Therefore it is possible to write about a body of religious and ethical principle shared by almost all Americans. This chapter and the one which follows are concerned with the general outlines of these principles, and with how these religious and moral ideas govern life in America.

Civilization grows out of religion: the morals, the politics, the economics, the literature, and the arts of any people all have a religious origin. Every people, no matter how savage or how civilized, have some form of religion: that is, some form of belief in a great supernatural power which influences human destinies. There had been no state in the whole history of the world which did not formally recognize the existence of God, or gods, until the Communists of Soviet Russia, and their satellite states, disavowed all religion and made atheism the official belief of the nation. But even the Russian Communists have not succeeded in stamping out religious faith in their own territories; indeed, the influence of Christianity is said to be increasing once more in Russia. And even the Communists have recognized that a people cannot exist without a body of moral principles. They have tried to substitute for Christianity a body of dogmas called "dialectical materialism." As Orestes Brownson pointed out in 1849, and as Arnold Toynbee has written very recently, Communism really is a kind of caricature of Christianity, borrowing certain of its moral affirmations, imitating its dogmas, and even appropriating some of its phrases. That makes Communism all the more dangerous: for the superficial similarities between Christian morality and the pretended Soviet morality sometimes delude Americans and people in other free states into thinking that Communism has high moral aspirations.

Moral Principle: The Nature of Man

Indispensability of moral principles

Whether or not a man is religiously-minded, he would be flying in the face of fact if he should argue that the element of religion in a nation's life can safely be ignored. The whole pattern in which we live our lives is formed by certain religious assumptions about the nature of God and the nature of man, even though we may have only a very vague notion of what the doctrines of religion are. The ideas of freedom, private rights, charity, love, duty, and honesty, for instance, all are beliefs religious in origin. These ideals also are discussed and advanced by philosophers, of course; but the original impulse behind them is religious. And in America, it is the Christian religion, nearly two thousand years old (or much older, when one includes the Jewish source of Christianity) and now worldwide in influence, which intimately affects our every action.

We cannot go deeply into theology in these two short chapters. But we propose to outline here certain essential Christian doctrines which have formed American character and society, and which are at the heart of the American cause. These beliefs are the fatherhood of God; the brotherhood of man; and the dignity of man. From these beliefs have developed Christian convictions as to how we should conduct our lives, how we should treat our fellow human beings, and what makes life worth living.

Awareness of God the Father

Christians know that there exists a supernatural power,

which we can perceive only dimly with our imperfect senses: a Supreme Being, the creator of heaven and earth, all-powerful. And that Supreme Being, God, made mankind, as He made everything else; but for man He has a special regard and a special mission. God created man in His own image. From time to time in history, God has revealed to man His power and His love. Slowly and painfully, an obscure desert people, the tribes of Israel, came to be aware of the nature of God; and through them, an understanding of God's majesty and intentions —so far as these things can be understood at all by mankind—was transmitted to the Christian world. To Moses on Mount Sinai, to prophets and saints, through miracles —and, most important of all to the Christian, through the person of Jesus of Nazareth, the Christ, the Redeemer— God made himself and his commandments known to mankind. In orthodox Christian doctrine, God became flesh in the person of Jesus, and suffered on the cross so that mankind might understand His nature and follow in His steps.

To man, God gradually made known His commandments and His intention for the human race. The Decalogue—the Ten Commandments delivered to Moses— commenced the instruction of man in how he must live with himself and with his neighbors. The teachings of the Hebrew prophets added to this body of knowledge of the divine will. And the life of Christ set the example for the conduct of all human life. Since the death of Christ, the meditations and actions of saints, and the reasoning of learned doctors, have added to Christian belief a great literature explanatory of God's nature and man's duty.

Original sin

Ever since the human race came into existence, the duty of man has been to strive to grow like unto God, his father. But man, an obstinate and perverse creature, repeatedly refuses or fails to follow in the steps of God. Every nation, every man and woman—even the best of us—commits evil at one time or another; some people spend most of their lives in doing evil. This failure of man to do good, to follow the commandments of God, is called sin; and sin has existed ever since mankind existed: so whether one considers the story of Adam and Eve to be literally true or a great myth (that is, a truth expressed in a story, disguised so as to make that truth the more striking), what the Christian calls Original Sin is simply a statement that men and women always have failed to follow the good consistently. Any reflective person is aware in his own daily life of how he frequently fails to be what he should: of how he is selfish, angry, obstinate, and vicious. We all sin; the difference between us in this is only a difference of degree.

God being perfect, that imperfection which we call sin is offensive in God's sight. Thus we all are offenders in God's eyes. Yet out of His love, He forgives the humble and contrite heart, and makes it possible for a man who seeks truth and righteousness to come to know Him.

Coming to know God is called salvation—being saved from the sins of this world. But deliberate turning away from God is called damnation—depriving one's self of the divine nature, denying one's own kinship with God, and sinking into the sub-human state of sin.

The world a place of trial

No man ever comes to know God perfectly in this world of time and space through which all of us pass for a few brief years. And no man, however vicious, ever quite succeeds in ignoring God in this world. Thus the world is a place of moral suffering, a place of trial; we are God's suffering servants, the Christian believes. Perfect happiness never can be attained upon this earth, in time and space as we know them, or in our perishing physical bodies. We are put into this world by God to be tested. Those who struggle to walk in the path God has pointed out may suffer greatly all their lives; but they will be rewarded by God through immortality, which is beyond time and space: what is called Heaven.

Those who reject God's commandments punish themselves, for they exile themselves forever from God's sight; this is called Hell. For this little worldly existence of ours, the Christian believes, is not our be-all and end-all. Every human being possesses an immortal soul. Through God's infinite grace, and by compliance with God's decrees, any person may win through this world of suffering to a peace beyond all understanding, an immortality which is purged of the sins and flaws of the world we now know.

Souls

Every person has a soul, a distinct essence. That soul is precious to God. Though all sinners, still all of us are the children of God, and able to earn His love, if we do not turn our faces away from Him. We all are brothers in sin; but God has commanded us to be brothers in righteousness also, and to treat one another as brothers. This the Christian calls kinship in Christ. Every human being here below is our brother, in a mystical sense: in the sense that we all are the spiritual sons of God.

Mystical brotherhood

Now men are brothers only in this mystical, spiritual kinship in Christ. In any literal sense, we are not flesh-and-blood brothers, or even thirty-second cousins. And we are enjoined to treat as brothers all the millions of our fellow human beings only because we all have the same spiritual father, God. If there were no God the Father, there could be no brotherhood of man. If God is denied, then men and women merely are bitterly competing little organisms, with no moral obligations to one another. They are not brothers, but fierce rivals.

Human dignity

This creature called man, who contains a spark of immortal life which is his personality, possesses dignity. That dignity is conferred upon him by God; and without God, there can be no human dignity. By "the dignity of man," Christians mean that every living person is entitled to be treated as a son of God, with respect for his personality. No matter how debauched or hideous or stupid a man may seem, he is entitled to certain rights and privileges, to be treated with a certain dignity, because he *is* a man and therefore a son of God, a brother in Christ. Few of us seem dignified in the ordinary conduct of life; nevertheless, our humanity entitles us all to be treated by our fellows as something better than animals. We have no right to treat our fellow human beings as if they were beasts; we owe even the least lovable of them our mercy and our charity. For there is in every one of them an immortal spirit, which comes from God; and if we treat them with indignity, in some sense we are insulting God.

Natural rights

From this concept of the dignity of man—a dignity which exists only through our relationship with God—there has grown up a recognition of what are called "natural rights." These are the rights which all men and women are entitled to: rights which belong to them simply because they participate in human dignity. There are other rights in our world: rights conferred by society at large, or by certain political and economic and social groups. These latter are man-made rights. But natural rights are rights which originate in the nature of every man—the character and personality given to men by God, the privileges that come from the fatherhood of God and the brotherhood of man. Everyone is entitled to possess these rights, no matter how strong or how weak he is, no matter how rich or how poor, no matter how civilized or how savage, no matter how famous or how humble.

Precisely what these rights are never has been entirely agreed upon, even among professed Christians. The medieval philosophers of the church debated for centuries on the character and extent of these rights: St. Thomas Aquinas's description of the rights of nature is one of the more important. Richard Hooker, an English theologian, discussed natural rights and natural laws in the sixteenth century, and his writings greatly influenced subsequent English and American opinion. John Locke, in the seventeenth century, said that there are three primary natural rights, "life, liberty, and property." In America, Thomas Jefferson, in the Declaration of Independence, made these rights "life, liberty, and the pursuit of happiness." Edmund Burke, perhaps the greatest modern political thinker, when he criticized the confused notions of natural right then popular among the French revolutionaries, went on to say that there are certain true and abiding natural rights, though they cannot always be set down independently and without qualification. Among them, he wrote, men have a right to live by law, for law is made to benefit them. "Men have a right to live by that rule; they have a right to do justice, as between their fellows, whether their fellows are in public function or in ordinary occupation. They have a right to the fruits of their industry, and to the means of making their industry fruitful. They have a right to the acquisitions of their parents; to the nourishment and improvement of their offspring; to instruction in life, and

31

to consolation in death." But, Burke added, "Men have no right to what is not reasonable, and to what is not for their benefit."

Natural duties

Generally speaking, Christians seem agreed that every right is joined to a corresponding duty. For every right we receive from God, we have a duty toward God; for every right of ours which other men respect, we are bound to respect the rights of other men. Natural "rights" are the things which our fellow human beings are forbidden to do to us or take away from us, under the laws of God. Every man has the right to charity, if he needs charity; but he also has the duty of laboring as best he can for himself, and of helping others if he can. Every man has the right to life; but he also has the duty of respecting the lives of others. A man may forfeit his natural rights by abuse: thus the thief forfeits the right to charity, and the murderer forfeits the right to life.

These natural rights impose upon all men and women certain limits and duties. We have no right to take another's life except to save our own or others' lives. We have no right to take away another's possessions without his consent, except when he has refused to pay to his neighbor or his community what he justly owes. We have no right to abuse, beat, torture, and debase other human beings: for they have a God-given right to dignity. And we have the great duty declared by Jesus in the Sermon on the Mount: to do unto others as we would have others do unto us.

Thus natural laws and natural rights and natural duties all are part of a divine plan for human destiny. They are the laws and rights and duties which arise from the enduring nature that God has given to human beings. The Christian believes that human nature does not change: the character of man in this world always will be what it is now, to the end of time—a mixture of good and evil. Therefore these natural rights and duties always will endure. It is better for a man to die than to surrender his natural rights or to ignore his natural duties. And this Christian concept of right and duty lies at the foundation of American society and government.

Impossibility of worldly perfection

Human nature will not change so long as this world endures, the Christian thinks. Good and evil always will be a war in human nature. And as human nature never will be perfected in the mortal world, so human society never will be perfected this side of eternity. It is our Christian duty in this world always to fight for the right: but we are not to expect that we ever shall succeed in establishing the perfect society or in developing the perfect man. It takes all our energies merely to keep evil in check, or to make modest progress in human affairs from time to time. Perfection exists only beyond space and time, in the kingdom of God: in what is called Heaven.

Thus the destiny of man, as son of God, will be completed only in a timeless and spaceless realm beyond the limits of our little world. Man is made for eternity. Because of the sins which we inflict upon ourselves, we suffer in this world; but that suffering will be wiped away by an existence in immortality, if we choose to love and obey God. As fleshly creatures, we are not made for perfection; it is only when we "put off mortality" that we can love and understand and share the perfection of God. It is one of the punishments of our sins that we would not love a perfect human nature, or a perfect society, even if we found such things in this little world of ours. Man as we know him, "the average sensual man," is perpetually discontented: he lusts after whatever he seems to lack. Whatever life he is living, the grass always seems greener on the other side. He is naturally envious and rebellious and proud. If ever the average sensual man—or any one of us—found himself, untransformed by death and immortality, in the perfect society, he would set to work at once abolishing that perfect society: for mortal man always is bored with what does not change. If ever the average sensual man—or any of us—found himself, untransformed by death and immortality, confronting the perfect human being, he would envy and perhaps destroy that human perfection. Precisely that was the fate of Jesus Christ, to be slain by those he had come to save. Here on earth, we crucify perfect things. It is only in another world than this that we shall love perfection and become part of it.

Therefore Christianity teaches men resignation: not to expect perfection in this world. But it also teaches men hope: aspiration to attain immortality and perfection, in another realm, through following the path which God has pointed out. And it reminds men that their duty is always to work for their own salvation and for the sake of their fellow men, even though no man ever will be perfectly happy in this world of ours.

Summary of Christian doctrine

In essence, then, the Christian faith is this. God exists, a stern judge but a loving father to all mankind. Man has been made in God's own image; but man, an imperfect image of God, torments himself by his tendency to sin. The world is always a battleground between good and evil in human nature. All men are brothers in spirit, because they have a common spiritual father, God; and they are enjoined to treat one another as brothers. Because they are made in the image of God, and are brothers in Christ, they possess human dignity. From this human dignity come rights peculiar to man which no one morally is free to violate. The revelations by God establish the way in which men are to live with one another. Justice and peace and charity all flow from God's commandments, given in a spirit of love. Christ will redeem from sin the man who accepts Him as savior. The reward of loving obedience to God is eternal life, perfection beyond this world. The self-punishment of defiant sin is never to know God: and thus to lose immortality. Human nature and society never will become perfect in the course of history. Yet God's love rules the world; and happiness, if we are to find it at all in this life, comes from doing God's will. As the essence of man is more than merely mortal, so the destiny of man is more than merely human. The spirit will survive the flesh, and when the end of all earthly things arrives, those who love God shall find a peace that the mortal world never knows. Men who expect to create a heaven upon earth, in defiance of the laws of man's nature and the revelation of God, can create only a hell upon earth.

Such is the Christian creed. Whether one subscribes to this religious faith or not, indisputably this is the religious framework upon which American society is built. Christan morality is the cement of American life; and Christian concepts of natural law for man, natural rights for man, and necessary limitations to human ambitions all govern our politics and even our economic system. That all Americans do not always abide by Christian teachings scarcely needs to be confessed. The immediate disciples of Christ did not always abide by all of Christ's teachings: for human nature is flawed, enslaved periodically or regularly to sin, and if the spirit is willing, still the flesh is weak. Our American society is far from perfect. Yet it is a society that works, and which ensures a tolerable measure of order and justice and freedom to men and women; as human societies go, it is a very high achievement. Our American order and justice and freedom would not be possible at all without the framework of religious and moral principle that we have described in the preceding pages.

Communist caricature of religion

Now this whole body of religious and moral principle is under attack by the revolutionary totalitarians of the twentieth century. The enemies of the American cause

36

dissent radically from the Christian concept of God's nature, human nature, human destiny, natural rights, and the moral rules which govern society. The official doctrine of the Nazis, for instance, repudiated Christianity—although admitting the existence of a Supreme Being, or at least of powers more than human—and rejected those concepts of human dignity and natural rights which are so closely interwoven into our view of life and our society. The horrors of the Nazi concentration camps were justified, in the Nazis' argument, by their denial that men are bound by any Christian moral laws: strength, in the Nazi view, was the only source of morality.

The Communists also repudiate Christian teaching, in some respects even more thoroughly than did the Nazis. They are thoroughgoing atheists, for one thing, substituting an abstract "The People" for God. It is not God's will that must be done, in the Communist ideology, but The People's will. In other respects, however, the Communists' doctrines are perversions of Christian doctrines, and sometimes even seem closely to resemble Christian belief, to the uninformed. Christianity, for instance, teaches that all men are equal in the sight of God— though in no other way. Communism teaches that even though there is no God, men ought to be equal in a complete political and economic sense in this world. Christianity also teaches that we owe one another charity, because we are brothers in Christ. Communism teaches that though Christ was an impostor, no man ought to have more than another, and therefore Com-

munist society will take away possessions from one man
and give to another. Christianity, moreover, teaches that
after life is over, and the end of all things has come, then
those who love God shall attain a heavenly perfection.
Communism, for its part, teaches that by revolution and
compulsion the perfect society shall be established here
on earth, and all men shall be perfectly happy, free to
"hunt in the morning," in Marx's words, "fish in the after-
noon, make love in the evening, and criticize at dinner
just as they please"—a child's dream of pleasure.

But these Communist ideals are a caricature of Christian principles. Cut off from their roots, these shadowy
copies of Christian aspirations have led only to a hell
upon earth. Although the Communists have preached
brotherhood, in practice they have murdered many millions of innocent people. Although the Communists have
praised absolute equality, they have established absolute
despotism. Although the Communists have aped Christian charity in words, they have resorted to theft and
confiscation in actuality. Although the Communists have
promised Utopia, they have delivered whole nations to
mortal torment. Although they have talked unendingly
of peace, they have thriven by war.

Such is the result of supposing that men will be virtu-
ous and good after they have denied the fatherhood of
God and the brotherhood of man. The Christian principles which sustain American society are not always
observed in America. But they never are entirely forgotten. They breathe life into our nation; they make us
truly human. They are sound principles, sound in de-

scribing the nature of God and the nature of man. Behind them is a great weight of authority and tradition and practice. Upon them, even more than upon our political and our economic theories and institutions, rests the American cause.

CHAPTER 4

Moral Principle: Church and State

American toleration

Complete toleration of religious belief and freedom of worship prevail throughout the United States. *Toleration* of all religious convictions, and toleration even of disbelief in any religion; but not indifference to religion: such is our national policy. The first clause of the First Amendment to the Constitution of the United States runs, "Congress shall make no law respecting an establishment of religion, or prohibiting the free exercise thereof." This provision is binding only upon the federal government, as distinct from the state governments; but nearly all the state constitutions contain similar provisions, and none of the states now has an established church.

American Constitution on religion

And this first clause of the First Amendment was intended to shelter religion, not to hamper churches. Because from the beginning America's population con-

40

sisted of Christians of many sects, with a sprinkling of Jews and people of other faiths, it would have been impractical and unjust for Congress to have established any one denomination as the state church. The majority of the framers of the Constitution were Episcopalians, but there were also Congregationalists, Presbyterians, Quakers, Unitarians, Methodists, Baptists, Catholics, and a few Deists—notably Jefferson and Franklin— among the founders of the Republic. Not one of our early statesmen was a professed atheist; and all of our presidents, with the possible exception of Jefferson, have publicly professed faith in Christian doctrines. (Jefferson drew up privately his own version of what he believed to be the direct teachings of Christ, the "Jefferson Bible"; and though unconvinced of the divinity of Jesus, he was profoundly attached to Christian morals.) From the first, then, we have been a Christian nation.

Jefferson once wrote to the Bey of Tunis, a Moslem ruler, that "the United States is not a Christian nation." By this, Jefferson meant that there being no establishment of religion in America, a Mohammedan ruler was not debarred by his own religion from dealing with the United States. In that sense, truly, the American government does not avow any particular religious creed. But, as Justice Story wrote in 1833 concerning the First Amendment to the Constitution, "The general if not the universal sentiment in America was, that Christianity ought to receive encouragement from the state so far as was not incompatible with the private rights of conscience and the freedom of religious worship." This view has been sustained by the federal Supreme Court down to our day. As Justice Douglas wrote in a Supreme Court decision of 1951, "We are a religious people whose institutions presuppose a Supreme Being. We guarantee the freedom to worship as one chooses. We make room for as wide a variety of beliefs and creeds as the spiritual needs of man deem necessary. . . . When the state encourages religious instruction or cooperates with religious authorities by adjusting the schedule of public events to sectarian needs, it follows the best of our traditions."

In many ways, we publicly recognize the authority of religious principle. The sessions of our Congress and our state legislatures open with prayers. We exempt the property of churches from taxation. We exempt ministers of religion from military service. We proclaim a national day of Thanksgiving religious in inspiration. We allow various expenditures of public funds for certain purposes friendly to religion. We swear oaths in courts on the Bible. Our official pledge of allegiance to the flag and the Republic now includes the words, "one nation, under God." Many of our oaths of office include acknowledgement of God's sovereignty. As a people, we feel that any just political authority must be consecrated in God's sight.

This sense of the religious foundation of our nation, accompanied by complete toleration of legitimate worship and private conscience, does not, of course, mean that we endure religious fanaticism in action, or that we refuse to prosecute acts which we consider immoral or harmful to society merely because they are committed under the name of religion. When a religious sect or a private believer actively violates the laws of the land, we do not hesitate to take stern steps to restrain such people. But in America any man can hold such religious views, or irreligious views, as he chooses, so long as he does not attempt to force those views upon others and so long as in his actions he does not violate the law.

This combination of complete toleration of opinion with national attachment to religious principle is very rare in the world. Most nations either recognize—formally or implicitly—a state religion, or else disavow religious truth altogether. Such a harmony between church and state is one of the principal achievements of American society, and no powerful religious body in America desires to alter this situation. Americans, then, may take pride in being the most tolerant of people—tolerant without sacrifice of religious conviction. We are a Christian nation—or, as some prefer to say, a Judeo-Christian nation—that observes religious principles in its public acts, though enforcing religious convictions upon no one.

Toleration abroad

In our dealings with other people, we have been scrupulously tolerant of religious beliefs and establishments. When, in 1846 and subsequent years, we occupied the region that is now the southwestern United States—and had been Mexican territory—it was inhabited almost entirely by Roman Catholics; but though Protestantism greatly predominated in the United States, we interfered in no way with Catholicism there; we respected church properties and religious convictions, as earlier we had in our purchase of Louisiana. When we occupied, in 1898, the Philippines, Guam, and other territories formerly Spanish, we were equally tolerant. In our present occupation of Japan, we have left the Buddhist and Shinto temples unmolested. Our troops in Europe have been careful never to intervene in religious matters. We maintain cordial relations with Moslem, Buddhist, Hindu, and even irreligious states and princes.

This does not mean that as a nation we have been indifferent to religious belief, or hostility toward religious belief, throughout the world. On the contrary, we have quickly extended refuge to fugitives from religious or irreligious persecution; when it has been in our power, we have employed every prudent means to discourage or moderate religious or irreligious fanaticism in other countries. The Nazi persecution of the Jews was one of the principal causes of our eventual declaration of war against Germany, and the Communist persecution of Christians in eastern Europe is a principal reason for our alliances with other nations to restrain the Soviets. There are circumstances—such as a Communist invasion of western Europe, accompanied by a threat to the very existence of Christian churches—under which, undoubtedly, we would fight to defend the religious convictions that we share with Christendom and Jewry, even though American churches and American material interests might not be immediately involved.

44

Moral Principle: Church and State

Not indifferent to religion

But this does not mean that our diplomacy is governed by preference for one religion over another, or even by a regular hostility toward irreligious governments. Ever since President Washington uttered his Farewell Address, we Americans have recognized that it is neither right nor expedient for us to dictate, in politics or in religion, to the rest of the world. We believe that—except for extreme cases of persecution which seem to violate the whole body of natural law—every nation must be left to follow the dictates of its own religious creed. Powerful though the United States is today, not even America has the strength—let alone the wisdom—to sit in judgment upon every theological and moral question raised in Europe and Asia and Africa. If foreign powers engage in policies which many of us may consider intolerant or immoral, still we do not feel entitled to act against those powers unless their policies contravene international agreements to which we are party, or unless those policies immediately menace the very foundation of religious and moral order in the world. Though we all in a sense, as individuals, are our brothers' keepers, as a political power the United States has not been appointed the keeper of the world's conscience. The toleration which we practice at home extends also to our foreign policy. From month to month, many things are done under the sun which Americans, as a nation, tend to think wrong; but the Republic of the United States, not caring to become a Don Quixote among the nations, generally does not try to set other nations in the path of righteousness. Great states, like private persons, must seek out their own salvation. As a world power, then, we are not a self-righteous nation; or, at worst, we try not to be.

Positive law not identical with moral law

Simply because an unjust act is committed in the affairs of nations, we are not obliged to try to set matters right: if we tried anything of the sort, we should become international busybodies, and should be disliked as all busybodies are disliked. It is only when our great national interests or the sources of modern civilization are threatened that we feel justified in using our national power to enforce the rules of international law. And even then, we rarely have intervened except at the urgent request of some international body or close ally. The observance of moral principles in international affairs, as in private life, must depend principally on voluntary and habitual obedience to the moral order, persuasion, and the force of public opinion. Just as we do not and can not station policemen in our homes to make sure that everyone behaves decently, so we do not and can not act, we Americans, as a moral police force zealously watching and admonishing foreign governments. Nationally, we are ruled by Christian principles; but Christian nations, like Christian persons, need frequently to recall the Christian doctrine, "Judge not, that ye be not judged." A Christian is not under the illusion that he can stamp out evil, forever, by using force. And thus a

Christian nation which understands its own religion cannot set up as a permanent censor and regulator of the ways of other states. It would be an un-Christian policy to compel other peoples to behave in what we Americans, at any particular moment, might take to be the Christian way.

There are many international concerns, then, in which Americans—though Christian in belief—do not presume to enforce obedience to strict Christian morals. This is no less true in our domestic concerns. Since our Republic was founded, we have made few attempts to write Christian dogmas into our statute-books. Some fundamental principles of morality, essential both to Christianity and to any decent civil social order, are to be found in the laws of the federal government and of every state, it is true: the prohibitions and penalties concerning murder, assault, robbery, and fraud, for instance. But such laws are common to all civilized people, with the partial exception of certain modern totalitarian states. No decent society could subsist without them; in this sense, all law is the reflection of certain great moral convictions. These fundamentals aside, however, we do not often attempt to regulate by law the complexities of private morality. In America, a man may stay within the law and yet do a considerable number of immoral things. He may lie, seduce, neglect his duties, waste his life, denounce his God, and yet run small risk of ever going to prison. He may be sensual, selfish, envious, and arrogant, and yet never come within the jurisdiction of our courts. He may break several of the Ten Commandments, and yet go scot-free all his life. The law of the state, in short, does not take cognizance of many failings which Christians regard as sinful. In most matters, we Americans do not try to regulate the details of moral behavior through statute and law-court. We do not try to make our law-code identical with the Christian code of ethics. We restrict the operation of our positive laws to those essential matters of public security which cannot be neglected without immediate danger to the whole fabric of civilized society.

This attitude toward the role of positive law—which we share with Britain and with many European states —is not anti-Christian or un-Christian. It is simply a wise recognition of the fact that if the political authority tries to do everything, it will end by doing nothing well. In most matters of private conduct and personal relationships, the state cannot intervene wisely or successfully; for judges and policemen are only human beings, with limited time and limited intelligence, and they are busy enough already, endeavoring—with only partial success —to enforce the bare essentials of public morality. And no nation can, or should, appoint half its population as judges and policemen to watch and reprimand the other half. Politics, it is said, is the art of the possible. Practical morals, too, is the art of the possible. It simply is not possible for political authority to enforce Christian morality, or any other sort of morality, in the everyday concerns of every man and woman. The regulation of ordinary conduct has to be left to private conscience, the influence of habit, custom, and example, and fear and respect for the opinions of one's neighbors.

By restricting itself to enforcing—as best it can—a few moral principles of general and inescapable concern, a political state does not repudiate Christian teaching. On the contrary, only by such a prudent restraint of its own authority can any just government uphold Christian morality. For a state which should arrogantly try to do what no state can do successfully—which should try to regulate every detail of private conduct on some absolute moral plan—soon would become a thoroughly un-Christian state. Even to commence such a course of action, the state would have to employ a crowd of spies, informers, and insufferable inspectors; even to begin to enforce its decrees under this system, the state would have to rely upon an army and a police force greater than even those now possessed by Soviet Russia.

Our American laws, then, are a reflection of moral law, and especially of Christian moral belief. But they are not the whole of moral law or of Christian morality. They settle for the possible: for what the political authority can undertake with reasonable efficiency and reasonable regard for private freedom.

So when we hear, within the United States or abroad, superficial reproaches about the American failure to make Christianity work in practical politics, we need make no shamefaced apologies. No nation in all history ever succeeded in making, through the judge and the policeman, its religion or its moral code the inflexible

49

law of the land. When such doctrinaire experiments have been tried, they have been catastrophic failures. All men and women are fallible, even the best of them; and many men and women are not well disposed. All that the law can do, in any country, is to maintain a tolerable balance of order and justice and freedom. The law cannot reconstitute human nature; it can only protect most decent human beings, most of the time, against the minority of indecent human beings. The morals and the laws of the United States, like those of other nations, cannot be fairly measured against some impossible standard of absolute perfection. That perfect justice and that perfect morality never have existed among men.

American Republic and religious teachings

But measured by any reasonable standard—by the yardstick of history or in the scales of twentieth-century justice—the American Republic has succeeded astonishingly well in applying Christian religious and moral principles to the governing of men. The United States has a government of laws, not of men, in which enduring rule—not personal caprice—is the supreme authority. The United States has a regard for charity, honesty, and human dignity unexcelled anywhere in the modern world. The United States has a system of justice founded upon the recognition of a justice more than human. The United States has a working political organization which makes right, not mere expediency, its aspiration. The United States enjoys a measure of toleration, public and private, almost unique in history. The United States has sound security of life and property; regular redress for serious wrongs; and a domestic peace possible only because most Americans continue to believe in the Decalogue, the preachings of the prophets, the teachings of Christ, and the reasonings of the great divines.

In the United States, the depredator generally does not go unpunished, and the unfortunate generally does not go to ruin. No nation has any right to be smug; for every nation's performance always falls short of that nation's duties. Yet, judged comparatively, America has some reason to be proud of her obedience to religious and moral truths. There always is immense room for improvement, anywhere. America's union of religious conviction with practical policy, nevertheless, has been as successful as most marriages can hope to be. Surely the fierce totalitarian regimes of our age have no just claim to say, Pharisee-like, to America, "I am holier than thou."

CHAPTER 5

Political Principle:
Ordered Liberty

Foundations of American republicanism

The United States of America is a federal republic: a federation of states governed by written constitutions. A part of the American political system is almost peculiar to the United States, particularly the checking and balancing of powers and interests by an elaborate system of enduring laws. But the political theories and customs which support our political institutions are very ancient in origin, most of them, and not peculiar to America.

Our constitution is republican—that is, designed to secure the public good through the sharing of political power among many people. The framers of our federal Constitution had in mind, as a model for American government, the ancient Roman republic, and Roman law and institutions still may be discerned in the structure of our government. And they also had in mind—so much at the back of their minds, indeed, that it formed the basis of most of their political opinions—the political experience of England, and English political philosophy.

Thus our American governments had for their foundation the English common law, English constitutional practice, and English political theory; and to their English legacy the founders of our Republic added Roman features.

American politics not abstract

Unlike the leaders of the French Revolution, the founders of the American Republic were not abstract theorists. (An acute German observer, Frederick Gentz, perceived the difference between the American and French experiments at the end of the eighteenth century, and pointed out that while the American Revolution was intended to secure in a practical fashion the American institutions and rights which already existed, the French Revolution was an attempt to turn a nation upside down and create something which never before had existed.) The signers of the Declaration of Independence and the framers of the Constitution did not create a republic out of whole cloth. Liking America much as they found it, they overturned English rule chiefly so that they might simply preserve the justice and order and freedom which the American colonies had long enjoyed. They were not creating Utopia; what they aimed at was the preservation, the conservation, of the rights and benefits they had inherited from their forefathers.

Thus when we speak of the theories which underlie our constitutions here in America, we do not mean a set of abstract doctrines flimsily constructed overnight to support some brand-new political system. By American political theories, rather, we mean those assumptions, bound up with certain moral principles, which Americans feel have been tested by many centuries of civilized experience—some of that experience here in America, most of it in Europe. For the most part, American political theories were developed from the combination of the theological and moral principles discussed in preceding chapters with the practical working of the European and English and American civil social order in history. Washington and Hamilton, Adams and Morris, Jefferson and Madison, knew history thoroughly. They were aware of the intricate process by which men had learned to live together in justice and order and freedom. They knew of the many mistakes which states had made, and of old political institutions which had proved themselves beneficial. They were acquainted with the growth of common law and constitutional government in England, and with the experience of colonial Americans in free institutions. Even the more radical among the founders of American government, like Thomas Jefferson, looked steadily to the past for guidance. Realizing that politics is the art of the possible, they settled for sound security in social institutions. They were not closet-philosophers, vainly pursuing the vision of a perfect society independent of human experience.

They knew political philosophy, as well as history and law. They had read, many of them, Plato and Aristotle, Cicero and Seneca, St. Augustine and Dante, Sir

Edward Coke and Richard Hooker, John Locke and Edmund Burke. They knew the writings of Kames and Blackstone and other legal theorists. But they were not bookish in the bad sense of that word: they did not divorce theory from practice. In their own careers they had united the authority of social custom with the authority of great books. They respected the wisdom of their ancestors. Especially they respected religious wisdom: nearly all of them had been brought up on the King James Version of the Bible, and most of them were intimately acquainted with the English Book of Common Prayer. Thus their political assumptions were compounded of Jewish religious doctrines, Christian teachings, classical philosophy, medieval learning, and English literature. And they were accustomed to testing these assumptions by reference to the historical experience of the ancient world, medieval society, English social development, and the American colonial experience. Out of such materials came the framework of our American Republic. We are a modern nation only in a restricted sense.

Three cardinal ideas of Western politics

Now in the political beliefs of what we call "Christian civilization" or "Western civilization"—of which American civilization is a part—there are three cardinal ideas: the idea of justice, the idea of order, and the idea of freedom. These three great concepts are the cement of American society. These three ideas dominated the minds of the founders of our Republic, and they are the principles which underlie American politics nowadays. These concepts of justice and order and freedom have been derived from Jewish and classical and Christian and European thought and experience. They are not peculiarly American; but they are essential to American social existence, and they have attained a high degree of practical expression in American life. They make possible the ordered liberty which is among the chief justifications of the American cause.

Meaning of justice

"Justice" is the principle and the process by which each man is accorded the things that are his own—the things which belong to his nature. This concept the old Greeks and Romans expressed in the phrase "to each his own." It is the principle and the process which protects a man's life, his property, his proven rights, his station in life, his dignity. It also is the principle and the process which metes out punishment to the evildoer: which enforces penalties against violence and fraud. The allegorical figure of Justice always holds a sword. Justice is the cornerstone of the world—divine justice and human justice. It is the first necessity of any decent society.

Meaning of order

"Order" is the principle and the process by which the peace and harmony of society are maintained. It is the arrangement of rights and duties in a state to ensure that a people will have just leaders, loyal citizens, and public tranquillity. It implies the obedience of a nation to the laws of God, and the obedience of individuals to just authority. Without order, justice rarely can be enforced, and freedom cannot be maintained.

Meaning of freedom

"Freedom" is the principle and the process by which a man is made master of his own life. It implies the right of individuals, whether the members of a certain class or all the members of adult society, to make their own choices in most matters. A slave is a person whose actions, in all important respects, are directed by others; a free man is a person who has the right—and the responsibility—of deciding how he is to live with himself and his neighbors.

American polity

Some dominations have order without justice or freedom; these we usually call tyrannies. Other dominations have freedom—for a while—without justice or order; such conditions we call anarchy. The founders of the American Republic, equally detesting tyranny and anarchy, determined to establish an enduring political constitution which would recognize the claims of justice, order, and freedom, and which would allow no excessive demands upon the part of any one of these three principles. Such a state, in which interests are balanced and harmonized by good laws, Aristotle had called a "polity." Our American polity is a regime of ordered liberty, designed to give justice and order and freedom all their due recognition and part. The founders of the Republic worked prudently with the materials they felt had been given to them by Providence: the American colonial experience of parliamentary government and local rights; the English legacy of common law and checks upon power; the Christian theories of natural law and natural rights; the classical ideal of a republic; the Old Testament morality which was the fundamental educational discipline of eighteenth-century Americans. They indulged in no political fantasies. The chief philosophical explanations of their aims and methods are *The Federalist Papers,* written by Hamilton, Madison, and Jay, and *A Defence of the Constitutions of Government of the United States,* written by John Adams. Their enduring monument is the Constitution of the United States.

Contrast with French Revolution

In the French Revolution, which began fourteen years later than the American Revolution, the revolutionary leaders—at least at the climax of the revolutionary movement—paid little heed to the ancient principles of justice, order, and freedom. They were not Christians; and, though they admired the political forms of Greek and Roman days, they felt no respect for the political traditions of their own country. Little influenced by a reverence for the wisdom of their ancestors, therefore, the chief French revolutionaries set out to establish what they thought would be a completely rational and completely new political order, independent of Providence and historical experience. In place of the old ideals of justice, order, and freedom, they shouted a novel slogan: "Liberty, equality, fraternity!" In their brave new world, the French reformers felt confident, all men would be absolutely free, perfectly equal, and happy in brotherly harmony. The duration of their dream was brief: fierce conspiracies and mass-executions gave the lie to their expected fraternity, a succession of cliques of intolerant politicians undid their expected equality, and the triumph of a dictator, Napoleon, put an end to the anarchic liberty they had celebrated. Having left Providence and historical experience and prudence out of their considerations, the French reformers passed speedily from the ineffectual monarchy of the Old Regime to the efficient tyranny of the Napoleonic Empire. The coming of Napoleon Bonaparte, indeed, was welcomed by the majority of the French; for though he ended freedom, he restored justice and order. And men cannot be content without justice and order.

The American Republic and its Constitution, in contrast, have endured with only slight changes for more than a hundred and seventy years. This remarkable permanence seems to be the product of the wisdom of the Republic's founders: they built upon the living rocks of justice, order, and freedom. Therefore it is worthwhile to examine what they understood by the terms justice, order, and freedom. By and large, the American cause today rests upon this same understanding of the meaning of those great ideas; for, perhaps more than any other people in the modern world, we are devoted to our national political traditions and venerate the documents in which they are expressed.

"To each his own"

The American revolutionary leaders, and the framers of the Constitution, believed that true justice can be obtained through recognizing the legitimate claim of each man to the expression of his own talents and his own personality—so long as his expression of talents and personality does not infringe unduly upon the rights and contentment of other people. "To each his own" means that every man has the right to seek the fulfillment of his own peculiar nature, to develop to the full the abilities which God has given him, within the bounds of charity and duty. Every man has the natural right to his own abilities and to what he has inherited from his forefathers. In the just state, the energetic man is protected in his right to the fruits of his endeavors; the contemplative man, in his right to study and leisure; the propertied man, in his rights of inheritance and bequest; the poor man, in his rights to decent treatment and peaceful existence; the religious man, in his right to worship; the craftsman, in his right to work. The just state, in short, will endeavor to ensure that no one shall take from another man what properly belongs to his personality, his station in life, and his material interests. The courts are arbiters when these claims seem to conflict. And no man shall be above the law: whatever a man's family, fame, wealth, or influence, he shall be expected to abide by the general rules of justice, as expressed in courts of law. The founders of the Republic were resolved that political and legal privilege—that is, exemption of certain powerful persons from the jurisdiction of many of the laws of the land, which then was practiced in nearly all the states of Europe—should not be endured in the United States of America. In America, justice should deal impartially with all claims; justice should be no respecter of persons, though justice should be the guardian of personal rights.

American concept of equality

These American statesmen, then, were convinced that men differ in character, talents, and needs. The function of justice is to assure to every man the rights which go with his particular character, talents, and needs. All men ought to be equal before the law; but the law is not intended to force upon them an artificial equality of condition. Justice does not exist in order to change men's natures; rather, justice's purpose is to help men fulfill the particular natures to which they were born. The founders of the Republic did not expect or wish that men ever would be equal in strength, cleverness, beauty, energy, wealth, eloquence, wisdom, or virtue. They did not want a society marked by any such dull uniformity of character. Such a society, in any event, would be impossible to create, they knew; and even were it possible, the result would be boredom and discontent for everyone in it. In one thing only ought men to be equal, here on earth: equally subject to the operation of just laws.

Jefferson, it is true, wrote in the Declaration of Independence that "all men are created free and equal." But the members of the Continental Congress who subscribed to that Declaration, and probably Jefferson himself, understood by this phrase that all men have natural rights to the development of personality and to equal justice under the law. No American leader of that day supposed that the helpless new-born baby is free, in any literal sense; obviously an infant is not born free, literally, but for a long while is in a condition of the most servile dependence. People are born free only in the sense that they are born to the right to seek what suits their nature. Similarly, the leaders of the young Republic were not so impractical as to think that all men are equal in mind or body or character or inheritance or environment; it was even more obvious in the eighteenth century than now that men are created highly unequal in all these respects. What they understood by the word "equal" in their Declaration of Independence is that all men, regardless of worldly station, enjoy a natural right to equal treatment under the law of the land: no man is privileged by nature to be exempt from the operation of justice. Justice, then, meant to the founders of the Republic the impartial administration of law to secure to every man the things which are his own by nature and inheritance. And this understanding of the nature of justice has endured unimpaired in American courts and American public opinion down to our day. Justice does not consist in forcing all men into an artificial and monotonous equality of worldly condition, through the power of the state; such a scheme would have seemed to the Republic's founders monstrously unjust. For the essence of justice is to assure by impartial adjudication that a man may keep whatever is rightfully his and pursue whatever his honest talents fit him for.

Order and classless society

What was the nature of order, in the eyes of the men who established the American political system? Proper order, they thought, is necessary to any civilized society. And order means that there must be a recognition of different functions and abilities among the members of society. Any society has its leaders. A justly ordered society will obtain good leaders; a badly ordered society will obtain unscrupulous and incompetent leaders. The founders of the American nation were republicans, but they did not believe for a moment that all men can be leaders; in any age, it is the nature of things that the few must lead and the many follow. They endeavored to ensure that the American Republic might choose its leaders wisely; and that those leaders' power might be hedged and bounded by wise constitutions and counterbalancing influences.

These statesmen of the early years of our country never meant to establish a "classless society." The classless society is the dream of Karl Marx and other nineteenth-century socialists. Classes always had existed in all lands, the Republic's founders reasoned, and classes are a social product of man's nature. There were many classes in their own America, and they expected that there always would be: fishermen, farmers, manual laborers, merchants, artisans, bankers, professional people, clergymen, landed proprietors, teachers, servants, soldiers, sailors, white trash, black trash, clerks, political administrators, shopkeepers, and yet more orders in society—most of them with a useful and inescapable function, and all of them probably destined to endure, as distinct elements in the nation, to the end of time. There was nothing immoral or obsolete about the existence of class, they felt: class was as natural in society as the separate functions of the brain, the heart, and the lungs in the human body.

Meaning of aristocracy

So they did not aspire to abolish class. What they disliked was not class, but *caste*: hereditary distinctions and privileges enforced by law. The granting of titles of nobility, accordingly, was forbidden expressly in the Constitution; and this violated no man's inherited rights, for there were no noblemen in America at the time of the Revolution. The founders of the Republic never aimed at the French vision of absolute equality, as preached by theorists like Condorcet. Though they could not abide caste, they heartily approved of "natural aristocracy"—the leadership of men of unusual talents and large resources. Old John Adams, in correspondence with Thomas Jefferson and John Taylor of Caroline, defined an aristocrat as any man who could influence two votes—his own and someone else's. An aristocrat, in other words, is a natural leader, qualified by intelligence, charm, strength, cleverness, industry, wealth, family, education, or some other resource to influence the opinions of his neighbors. Jefferson, in Virginia, as strongly supported the claims and rights of an aristocracy of nature as did Burke, in England. The leaders of American thought and politics knew that any society without honorable leaders must be a disorderly society. What they foresaw for the future of the Republic was not, then, the abolition of class and superior talents, but the employment of class and superior talents to the benefit of the commonwealth.

These American statesmen were neither pure aristocrats nor pure democrats. They distrusted both aristocracy and democracy, as unmodified forms of government. A satisfactorily orderly society, they argued, must consist of a mixture of aristocracy and democracy, a balancing and checking and harmonizing of the influence of wealth and private ability with the influence of numbers and popular desire. They wrote into the federal constitution and the state constitutions safeguards both against the power of wealth and the power of needy majorities; against the ambition of gifted men and the appetite of average men.

They feared the lust for power of the strong man; and they feared the lust for possessions of the poor man. They knew that some unusual men and some ordinary men, in any age, will abuse whatever powers they enjoy. So the founders of the Republic devised a system of constitutional laws—which will be more fully described in the chapter which follows—that would protect decent social order from either the autocrat or the mob, that would balance the interest and authority of one interest or class in state and nation against other interests and classes, that would provide a democratically-based society with a soundly aristocratic leadership.

"Without order, there is no living together in society": so the authors of the American political system had learned from the English political philosophers, and from their own century and a half of experience in the New World. As nations go, the American Republic has been amazingly orderly, with only one civil war in its history, no successful revolt since the Declaration of Independence, and very few violent protests against the conduct of government. Among the great states of the modern world, only Great Britain—if one excludes Ireland and the British Commonwealth and imperial possessions—has so enviable a record. Every man seeks order in his own life; he is miserable if he lacks it. And every nation that lacks order is bitterly unhappy. The American experiment in the keeping of order remains probably America's proudest just claim to high respect among the nations; it matters far more, for civilization and for American happiness, than the "American standard of living" about which we boast so frequently.

Specific nature of American liberties

Finally, the leaders of the new American Republic knew very well what they meant when they used the word "freedom." They thought it no paradox that true freedom is obedience to the laws of God. Legitimate freedom, they said, is the right of decent men, governed by conscience, to make their own principal choices in life. And by this they meant no vague abstraction called "Liberty" with a capital L. They were not anarchists, and they were not radical Jacobins. They did not convert their old, sensible, long-cherished English and American freedoms into a cloud-veiled goddess, before whom justice and order must yield pride of place. Most of them, having read John Milton, were well aware of those dangerous persons who "license they mean, when they cry liberty." A few of the American patriots, like Samuel Adams most of his career or Patrick Henry early in life, stood for an absolute and all-embracing liberty of every man to do as impulse bade him; but the great majority, led by prudent men like John Adams, Benjamin Franklin, James Madison, Gouverneur Morris, George Wythe, John Rutledge, James Wilson, John Marshall, Alexander Hamilton, and others—men of every party and faction—desired only a disciplined, traditional, moderate, law-respecting freedom.

Freedom, defined in the negative, is security against having things done to you that you do not wish to have done to you. The civil liberties which colonial America had long enjoyed were of this character; and they were derived from old English liberties, developed and secured over seven centuries. By what was called "a salutary neglect," the English government generally had left the colonists to manage their own affairs, in nearly everything, and thus the thirteen American colonies had grown accustomed to freedom in the conduct of their local concerns and their private lives. Only when the ministers of George III began to assert the absolute and abstract right of king and parliament to make laws for the Americans did the desire for American independence begin to make itself felt. The Americans no longer felt secure that things would not be done to them of which they might not approve; in short, they ceased to feel free. And having been long familiar with freedom, they were willing to risk death for the sake of keeping up that intimacy.

The Americans, therefore, in their petitions to the king of England, in their Declaration of Independence, and in their federal Constitution, did not make the extravagant claims to an unlimited and unhistorical liberty which infatuated the French revolutionaries. In the beginning of their struggle against English power, the colonists asked only that they be confirmed as participants in the long-established "rights of Englishmen." In the Declaration of Independence, they drew up a list of very specific rights to freedom which they felt had been violated or endangered by the king's ministers. In the "Bill of Rights," the ten amendments appended to the Constitution in the first years of the Republic, the American people set down a few definite liberties which expressed precisely what they meant by political freedom. They did not mean by freedom "the absolute right to do whatever we please, regardless of our religion, our duties, and our neighbors." They meant, very differently, certain old and valuable securities against having things done to them, by the state or by powerful men, which they would not relish having done to them. Freedom from interference with religious opinion and worship; freedom from arbitrary arrest; freedom from having troops quartered in one's house; freedom from cruel and unusual punishments; freedom from arbitrary censorship of the press and of speech; freedom from taxation without representation—such were some of the very practical and well-known liberties which they desired to secure. They did not ask for liberation from moral obligations, or from paying rents and debts and taxes, or from the jurisdiction of the courts. They did not ask for freedoms which no political power possibly can guarantee, like "freedom from fear" and "freedom from want." They asked only for the possible: the maintenance or restoration of certain traditional rights of Englishmen and Americans. Freedom, they knew, is not a possession which some prince or president can confer upon men as a gift: not true freedom. Real freedom must be created by individuals and communities. All that central political authority can accomplish is to promise not to abridge the freedoms which men have made for themselves, or which they receive as part of their birthright from God.

Unrestrained liberty

The founders of the Republic put no trust in absolute, unqualified Liberty. Unrestrained Liberty they thought as dangerous as unrestrained Power. Christian liberty and rightful civil freedoms must be balanced and bounded by the safeguards of conscience, custom, good order, and good constitutions. "O Liberty, what crimes are committed in thy name!" Madame Roland—who was one of the Girondist worshippers of Liberty—cried on her way to the guillotine in Paris. The American statesmen were resolved that, if they could prevent it, no crimes would be committed in Liberty's name in the United States. With few exceptions, their resolution has persisted among Americans down to our decade. Most intelligent Americans today agree with Dostoevski's observation that "If one begins with unlimited freedom, he will end with unlimited despotism." The American cause is not the cause of a revolutionary thirst for demolishing all obstacles to anarchic self-gratification. When the modern American, like the eighteenth-century American, uses the word "freedom," he means freedom under God, freedom under law, freedom justified by many years of national experience. "Men of intemperate mind never can be free," Edmund Burke wrote early in the French Revolution. "Their passions form their fetters." American freedom has been the liberty of temperate policies and temperate intellects.

American political equilibrium

Justice, and order, and freedom: the true polity, the really successful commonwealth, emphasizes equally all three of these. Now and then, in the history of the United States, we have erred by neglecting one of these principles, at some particular moment, or by over-emphasizing another, on a different occasion. Yet, taken all in all, the concepts of the founders of the Republic have endured with a strength and consistency most rare in the course of national destinies. Americans do not presume to argue, if they are wise, that their American institutions might be easily adapted to the needs and ways of other nations; nor that their commonwealth has functioned in every respect better than any other national state. Such self-praise is more liable to vex than to convert our neighbors. But when we hear this little failure of justice in Georgia, or that little neglect of freedom in New York, bewailed and denounced out of all proportion by critics of American institutions, at home or abroad, we have the right to appeal to the perspective of history. Historically judged, the American Republic has maintained a balance of justice and order and freedom for a century and three quarters which many nations have not been able to maintain as successfully for even a single year in the whole record of their affairs. Nearly all Americans, on nearly all occasions, can rely, if the necessity arises, upon obtaining impartial justice from the courts; upon being wholly secure in their persons and property through the solidity of American order; upon doing any reasonable thing they like without reprimand. The same could not be said for the glory that was Greece or the grandeur that was Rome.

CHAPTER 6

Political Principle:
The Federal Republic

Source of authority

"In questions of power," Thomas Jefferson wrote, "let no more be heard of confidence in man, but bind him down from mischief by the chains of the Constitution." The constitutions of the American commonwealth are intended—and have successfully operated—to restrain political power: to prevent any man or clique or party from dominating permanently the government of the country. Sir Henry Maine, the nineteenth-century historian of law, remarked that the American Constitution is the great political achievement of modern times. The American constitutional system reconciles popular government with private and local rights. It has been called "filtered democracy"—that is, the reign of public opinion chastened and limited by enduring laws, political checks and balances, and representative institutions. It combines stability with popular sovereignty.

It is one of the great premises of American political theory that all just authority comes from the people, under God: not from a monarch or a governing class, but from the innumerable individuals who make up the public. The people delegate to government only so much power as they think it prudent for government to exercise; they reserve to themselves all the powers and rights that are not expressly granted to the federal or state or local governments. Government is the creation of the people, not their master. Thus the American political system, first of all, is a system of limited, delegated powers, entrusted to political officers and representatives and leaders for certain well-defined public purposes. Only through the recognition of this theory of popular sovereignty, and only through this explicit delegation of powers, the founders of the American Republic believed, could the American nation keep clear of tyranny or anarchy. The theory and the system have succeeded: America never has endured a dictator or tolerated violent social disorder.

Pure democracy

But in asserting that all power comes from the people, the founders of the Republic had no intention of creating a direct or "pure" national democracy. Early American statesmen—and most of their successors—distrusted popular passions and appetites quite as much as they distrusted the ambitions of strong men. They intended to restrain both the mob and the autocrat. They were not under the illusion that most men and women are naturally good or wise; they knew that neither a great popular majority nor a clever and able minority is fit to be trusted with absolute power. They did not believe that the voice of the people is the voice of God. Although government must exercise considerable power in order to administer justice and defend the commonwealth, nevertheless that necessary power remains always potentially dangerous; it must be held in check by sound constitutions and customs, and by a balancing of the various interests and branches of government, every one of which ought to keep a jealous eye upon the others.

Meaning of federalism

Therefore the United States is not a centralized democracy. It does not have government from the top downward; on the contrary, it has government from the bottom upward. Strictly speaking, we have no national government: our government is *federal*, a union of states for certain explicit purposes of general benefit. Federation is very different from centralization. The theory of federation is this, that forty-eight sovereign states have conferred, of their own free will, certain powers upon the federal administration, to promote the interests of the several states and of the people within those several states. The United States are united voluntarily, and are united only for the purposes, and under the conditions, described in the federal Constitution. In the matters which most immediately affect private life, power remains in the possession of the several states; while within those forty-eight states, the people reserve to themselves, as individuals, control over most walks of life. The state governments, like the federal government, are hedged and checked by constitutions and public custom.

Limited government

Everywhere in America, individuals and private voluntary associations jealously reserve to themselves the rights of choice and action in those spheres of activity which most nearly affect the private person. The state touches these private concerns only upon suffrance, or not at all. Religious belief and affiliation are matters wholly of private choice; economic activity, by and large, is left to the will of individuals; social relationships are voluntary and private relationships; where one lives, and how, is not determined by political authority. Quite as much as in England, an American's home is his castle. A great many Americans live their lives through without ever conversing with a civil servant, or even saying more than good morning to a policeman. Americans have no official cards of identity, or internal passports, or system of national registration. Until 1941, America never experienced peacetime conscription into the armed forces. Nowhere in the world is the operation of government less conspicuous than in the United States. If an American citizen desires to abstain altogether from political activity, even to the extent of never voting, no one interferes with him; and for millions of Americans, their only direct contact with government is their annual submission of income-tax reports. Private life looms much larger than public life in the American commonwealth.

Even in those concerns which have been opened to

local or state or federal political activity, the theory persists that political authority operates only as a convenience to private citizens. The public schools, for instance, are intended simply to facilitate the education of young people, not to enforce the educational doctrines of central authority: although nearly all the states require that children should be schooled in some fashion, everywhere parents are free to educate their children privately, or in denominational schools, if they prefer such methods to enrollment in public schools. The American assumption is that education is primarily the concern of the family and the individual, not of the political state; and this frame of mind extends to many more activities in which the state acts as servant, rather than as master.

Territorial democracy

So in America the things in which people are most interested generally remain strictly within the jurisdiction of private life. And in matters of public concern, it is the American habit to keep authority as close to home as possible. The lesser courts, the police, the maintenance of roads and sanitation, the raising of property-taxes, the control of public schools, and many other essential functions still are carried on, for the most part, by the agencies of local community: the township, the village, the city, the county. American political parties, in essence, are loose local associations: the state and national party organizations are merely the reflections of local opinion in caucus and town meeting. This state of affairs is what Orestes Brownson, more than a hundred years ago, called "territorial democracy": popular local control over local affairs, accompanied by strict checks upon state and federal political power. In this sense, the American nation is genuinely democratic, keeping power in the hands of the people. And commonly Americans are more interested in local public affairs than in national political concerns: many more voters may turn out for a school-board election than for a senatorial or even a presidential election.

State governments

What the local community cannot do in the public interest, the state governments generally undertake; only a few matters of national importance are left to the jurisdiction of federal authority. In the courts, the great majority of civil and criminal cases are reserved to the state judges; education, health, and public charity are almost exclusively the concern of state governments, when they are not locally administered; road-building and utility-regulation, for the most part, are state functions; the states even have their own military organizations. Though every state is required to give full faith and credit to the acts of all the other states, still they may make what laws and experiments they please, so long as they do not contravene the few and specific limitations written into the federal Constitution. The American states, in short, are very like the Swiss cantons, autonomous for most purposes, and proud of their distinct identity. Many Americans continue to think of themselves as Virginians or Californians or Massachu-

77

setts men first, and citizens of the United States second. The belief in states' rights, the view of government which is called "particularism" or "regionalism," remains strong throughout the country.

Every state has its written constitution, usually more detailed than the federal Constitution, and intended—like the federal Constitution—to put strict limits to the exercise of political power. The state legislatures can draw up public acts only within the scope allowed by the state constitutions, as interpreted by the state supreme courts. Within each of the states, a balance is maintained among the executive, the legislative, and the judicial branches of government. The powers of state governors are limited to the administration of the laws and the vetoing—under certain conditions, differing from one state to another—of bills passed by the legislature; the state judiciary generally maintain their independence of both governor and legislature. As for the forty-eight legislatures, meeting annually or semi-annually, they too are subject to the American principle of limited and balanced powers: with only one exception—Nebraska, which has a one-chamber legislature—the state legislatures consist of an upper chamber, the senate, and a lower, the house of representatives or assembly. Generally speaking, the state houses of representatives tend to represent population, while the senates tend to represent area, rural constituencies usually predominating in the senates. To the enactment of most legislation, therefore, the consent of house of representatives, senate, and governor is necessary; while the state courts keep watch upon the constitutionality of legislation. The American public has a healthy prejudice against hasty, partial, and arbitrary law-making. In a number of states, the devices of popular initiative, referendum, and recall of public officers lie in reserve as further checks upon men in power.

Representatives

Anyone who wishes to understand American political theory and practice cannot do better than to sit in the gallery of a state senate or house of representatives. From such an observation-post, the meaning of the phrase "filtered democracy" soon becomes clear. Like the members of the national Congress, the members of the state legislatures are not delegates from their constituencies, but genuine *representatives:* that is, they sit in the legislature as men of independent judgment, in the tradition of English and American parliamentary usage. They are sent to the legislature not simply to be the mouthpieces of the voters from their respective districts, but rather to deliberate freely on the innumerable questions of the session; and, by and large, they tend to vote as they please and as they think best. Thomas Jefferson said that although most men are not competent to judge intelligently concerning particular political questions of the hour, nevertheless most men are quite competent to choose representatives qualified to determine such questions; and this remains the theory of American legislative bodies. The state legislatures, like the Congress, represent the popular will, but they endeavor to express that will prudently and conscientiously, and in obedience to the state constitutions. They constitute one of the chief filters of public opinion. On this burning question or that, the better judgment of state legislators may give way before popular agitation or the influence of a powerful lobby; yet throughout their history the state legislative bodies have succeeded, by and large, in reconciling popular demands with prudence and long views. Whatever the deficiencies of particular members of state legislatures, free government in America could not function properly without these representative institutions.

Federal government

The American federal government is an American state government writ large. The American President is a greater governor; the Congress, a more talented legislature; the Supreme Court of the United States, a tribunal with the same traditions and procedures as the state supreme courts. For the American states—thirteen of them, at least—are older than the federal government, and served as models for the federal organization. The federal administration is a common government, but not a supreme government: for in many things, the federal government has no authority, those matters being reserved to the states or the people of the states.

The first, second, and third articles of the federal Constitution define, respectively, the rights and duties of the legislative, executive, and judicial powers of the federal government. The legislative power, the Congress of the United States, is composed of two houses, the Senate and the House of Representatives: the first consists of two senators from each state in the Union, the second of representatives apportioned to each state on the basis of population. Thus the sovereignty of the several states is recognized in the Constitution's first article, for each state has the right to two senators, regardless of population: in the Senate, empty Nevada is as important as crowded New York City. In this, as in many other matters, the United States is not a "pure" democracy; what the framers of the Constitution intended and achieved was not unchecked popular rule, but a judicious balancing and checking of the different interests and states in the Union.

Legislative power

Until the Seventeenth Amendment was adopted, in 1913, indeed, United States senators were not chosen by popular vote at all, but by the legislatures of the states. The Senate is intended to serve as a kind of aristocracy in the federal government. The terms of senators are for six years; the Senate alone can try impeachments of federal officers; and the Senate alone confirms treaties negotiated by the President, and diplomatic appointments made by him. The United States Senate is the most powerful representative body in the world today, and—except for the British House of Lords—probably the most able and dignified.

The federal House of Representatives, a much larger body than the Senate, was intended to serve as the popular branch of the federal legislative power, more directly responsive to public opinion; and its members hold office for two years. The House of Representatives alone can originate bills for raising revenue—a prerogative copied from the colonial assemblies and the English parliament.

In Section Eight of the first article of the Constitution, the powers of Congress are stated explicitly; and, except for such extensions of power as have been granted by later amendments to the Constitution, all powers not specified in this section are reserved to the states or to the people of the states: thus the Congress is not a representative body with powers almost unlimited, like the English Parliament, but rather a limited assembly intended to exercise jurisdiction over certain well-defined matters. The Congress can raise taxes, declare war and peace, maintain armies and navies, borrow money, regulate foreign commerce, coin money, establish post offices and post roads, punish offenses against international law, constitute federal courts inferior to the Supreme Court, grant copyrights and patents, govern federal territories, and do a number of other things intended to promote the general welfare of the United States; but the Congress cannot intervene in the internal affairs of the several states, nor encroach upon the functions of the executive and judicial branches. Since the foundation of the Republic, the powers exercised by Congress have increased in some particulars; yet the Congress remains a legislative body of limited authority; it is not supreme over the nation.

Executive power

As for the President of the United States, the executive power of the federal system, he now is the most powerful man in the world; and yet his authority is even more severely hedged than is that of Congress. No American President ever has been a real dictator, even in time of war, and if the Constitution continues to function, no president ever will be absolute. Lincoln and Wilson and Franklin Roosevelt were the three Presidents whose war-time responsibilities gave them an authority greater than that comtemplated by the framers of the Constitution; yet even their emergency-powers could not have been exercised without the concurrence of the Congress, the federal courts, and the majority of the states. The American President may seem to people abroad to be almost a monarch; but at home he remains only the chief magistrate, more limited in his authority than are many European prime ministers.

Very often the political party to which the President happens to belong may be the minority party in both Senate and House of Representatives, since—unlike the prime ministers and premiers of European parliamentary systems—the American President is not a member of the federal legislative branch and is not chosen from Congress. In theory, the President is chosen, every four years, by a body of special "Electors," the Electoral College, who in their turn have been chosen by the people of the several states; but in actuality the Electoral College never has functioned as the framers of the Constitution intended, and the President really is chosen directly by the people of the several states, from among the two or three candidates for the presidency nominated by the chief American political parties.

The President is commander-in-chief of the American army and navy, general supervisor of the federal administration in civil matters, and head of the diplomatic service; he has large powers of pardon and reprieve, and may convene Congress in extraordinary session. As the activities of the federal government have grown, within the United States and abroad, the powers of the President have increased proportionately. Yet it is a remarkable fact that no President ever has endeavored to make himself absolute, and that most Presidents have deliberately restrained themselves in the exercise of their legitimate authority. Whenever a President has seemed to seek to increase his power unduly—as, for instance, when Franklin Roosevelt, during his second term in office, sought to obtain control over the Supreme Court through a bill to enlarge its membership—the Congress and public opinion have decided against him, no matter how popular such a President may have been otherwise. Although Congress has the constitutional authority to impeach and remove a President for treason, bribery, and other high crimes and misdemeanors, not a single President has been so removed, and only once—in the case of President Andrew Johnson—was impeachment ever undertaken. When one remembers that the President has no final authority above him—no king, as in the British system, and no permanent president, as in the French system—this record of probity and self-restraint among American Presidents becomes one of the highest achievements of politics in the history of civilization. The American President has powers nearly equivalent to those of the earlier Roman Emperors; but where the Roman system could show only a handful of just and able emperors in the course of centuries, the American system has enjoyed conscientious Presidents without interrupting since its inception—and a half-dozen of those Presidents have been men of the highest general abilities.

Judicial power

The third great division of the federal government, the judicial power, is dominated by the Supreme Court of the United States, consisting of nine experienced justices who hold office permanently, after appointment by the President. By Constitutional provision, the Supreme Court and the lesser federal courts decide on questions of interpretation of the Constitution; on cases arising under federal law and treaties; on cases affecting ambassadors, ministers, and consuls, and maritime law; on controversies involving the United States and the federal government; on controversies between different states of the Union, between a state and citizens of another state, between citizens of different states, and between American citizens and foreign states or citizens of foreign states. The great bulk of civil and criminal cases in America, however, are in the jurisdiction of the separate state courts.

Early in the history of the Republic, the Supreme

Court was secured in its extensive powers and high re-
pute by the strongest of all Chief Justices, John Marshall.
Ever since then, with only two or three passing exceptions, decisions of the United States Supreme Court have
been promptly and voluntarily obeyed as the law of the
land. In popular respect, the Supreme Court stands even
higher than the Congress and the President. From time
to time, the Supreme Court has handed down decisions
which were highly unpopular; yet those decisions almost always were accepted and enforced. No other
judicial body in all the world is so powerful and so rev-
erenced as is the Supreme Court of the United States.
For Americans feel that the Supreme Court, whether or
not they agree with its particular decisions at a particular
time, in the long run shelters and represents the American principle of liberty under law and the American
principle of a government "of laws, not of men."

In general, the Supreme Court has been the stern
defender of civil rights, of the rights of property, and of
the federal and state constitutions. Throughout most of
its history, the majority of justices have recognized the
principles of "natural law" as applicable to American
society, though there has been some weakening of this
belief within the Supreme Court and the other federal
courts during the twentieth century. In some periods,
the Supreme Court, in questions of constitutional interpretation and the division of powers, has tended to
favor the state governments against the federal government; and at other periods—particularly at present—it

has leaned toward interpretations which favor the federal government against the state governments. At almost all times the federal courts have acted to protect the individual citizen from encroachments upon his rights by the state or by arbitrary individuals and groups. It is this role of the Supreme Court and the other federal courts as protectors of justice, order, and freedom which has given the federal judiciary such an ascendancy over public opinion.

The federal courts have no armies and navies at their command; their decisions are executed merely by a few federal marshals, appointed by the executive branch. The justices of the Supreme Court are merely nine old men, ordinarily without wealth or even great personal popularity to reinforce their authority. Yet their decisions are obeyed—even by the strongest and most willful of Presidents—quickly and unquestioningly, in nearly every instance. Congress can remove certain classes of legal cases from their jurisdiction, as Congress did during the Civil War; but this Congressional power is very rarely exercised. President Andrew Jackson, angered by Chief Justice Marshall's opinion on one occasion, is said to have declared, "Justice Marshall has made his decision; now let him enforce it." But this attitude of defiance has been almost unique in American history, and President after President has bowed to—and executed—judicial decisions which ran contrary to his plans. There is no better illustration than this of the respect for just authority prevalent in the United States, and of the veneration in which the American Constitution is held by nearly everyone.

Vigor of the American political system

So the American political system endures to this day, through wars and civil emergencies, despite immense territorial and population growth in the nation, a system which successfully maintains justice and order and freedom by placing restraints upon power; by keeping sovereignty in the hands of the people, yet preventing mob-rule. Eighteen decades is a great while for any political system to thrive unaltered in essence; yet American constitutional structure, despite all the problems of twentieth-century society, still seems adequate to the needs of the American nation, and shows few signs of decay. Surely there are very few Americans who advocate any substantial change in the fundamental political institutions of their country—fewer, indeed, than there were seventy or eighty years ago. As Mr. Walter Lippmann suggests in his book *The Public Philosophy*, the present leadership of the United States among the nations thrusts upon the American nation unfamiliar problems of statecraft; but it appears probable that these challenges will be met without serious alteration of the American political foundations. Local rights will continue to be cherished even in the increasingly urbanized and industrialized new America; the states will continue to assert their sovereignty; and the three divisions of the federal government will continue to divide federal authority among them.

Political parties

Now the functioning of this constitutional system has been possible only through the work of free political parties in the United States. President Washington hoped that "faction," or political parties, might be unnecessary in the new Republic, but events proved otherwise. In order to undertake any intelligent political action, in order to chart any course for local or state or federal government, men and women must associate themselves in voluntary groups which we call political parties; if party is lacking, then power slips by default into the hands of private cliques or demagogues. By and large, the major American parties have been responsible, though loose-knit, organizations. In the early years of the Republic, the Federalist and Republican-Democratic parties contended against each other; in the years before the Civil War, the Whig and Democratic parties; since the Civil War, the Republican and Democratic parties. This contest, usually, of simply two large parties against each other has been very like the British experience with the Conservative and Liberal, and the Conservative and Labour, parties; small minority parties, "splinter" parties, do not seem to fit well into the structure of American or English politics. The chief European states, on the other hand, have been accustomed to the existence of perhaps a dozen rival parties, forming coalition governments from time to time. If the domination of two great parties possibly has resulted in a less vigorous expression of minority opinions in the United States, nevertheless the direction of public opinion into one or the other of two enduring groups has helped to give stability to the American political structure.

Two facts ought to be noted concerning these American parties: they are not "ideological," and they are not tightly organized. When we say they are not ideological, we mean that they are not fanatical; they do not adhere, ordinarily, to rigid political dogmas at whatever expense to practical consequences in the nation. When we say they are not tightly organized, we mean that they have no true central direction: the Republican party, or the Democratic party, takes whatever stand on a particular issue that the people "back home," the men and women who attend the village or precinct party caucus, think their party ought to take on that particular issue. The national party program, and the national party candidates, are determined by many thousands of little local meetings of interested citizens; and these little local meetings are given state-wide expression every two years, in most states, by state party conventions; and nation-wide expression, every four years, by national party conventions.

If, then, it sometimes is said that American parties seem to have no enduring principles, nevertheless we need to remember that neither do they have enduring fanaticisms and errors; and if sometimes it is said that American parties seem to have no permanent leaders, still we need to remember that neither do they have party dictators. Like all other aspects of American political existence, our parties are complex, diverse, cautious, and obedient to the American concept of "territorial democracy." Only once, in all American history, have our parties gone to war; and even then, in the struggle between the states, the alignment of forces was not clearly partisan, for many northern Democrats fought for the Union, and many southern Whigs fought for the Confederacy. Probably a certain vagueness about party doctrines is not a very high price to pay for political peace. Whatever their faults—and most of their old faults, such as the power of party bosses and the spoils-system in appointments to public office, are much diminished nowadays— our political parties have succeeded in enabling representative government to function freely among us. There are only three possibilities beyond moderate political parties: fierce factionalism, dictatorship, and anarchy.

American government and sound security

The founders of the Republic, and their inheritors, knew what might reasonably be expected of a good society: not Utopia, but a domination of tolerable justice and order and freedom. Commencing from sound philosophical postulates and well-understood historical experience, the leaders of the American nation have succeeded in fulfilling their reasonable hopes. Ours is a truly popular political system, in which the rights of private persons and minorities are protected from temporary majorities by sound constitutions and enduring rules of procedure. As well as any society ever can, probably, we have reconciled the claims of justice and order and freedom. Thinking Americans do not say that the American system of government necessarily is the best system of government for Austria, or Indonesia, or Abyssinia, or the whole world; they say only that it is the best form of government for the United States of America, given our moral and political and economic beliefs and our historical experiences. But they do commend it to other peoples as one successful type of polity, a prudent preference for sound security over dreams of Utopia. The federal republic of the United States is one of the principal proofs of the American cause.

CHAPTER 7

Economic Principle:
The Free Economy

Reasons for American belief in free enterprise

Political freedom and economic freedom, the great majority of Americans think, are bound together inseparably. Nor can freedom of religious opinion be altogether separated from freedom of economic life. This conviction that a free economy is a support of all freedom is one strong motive behind the American championship of what Marxists usually call "capitalism" and what more prudent thinkers usually call "free economic enterprise" or "a free economy."

There are other reasons for this American attitude. One of them is the belief that only a society which, by and large, is economically free can be a just society; for the just society is one in which each man may seek the things which belong to his nature; and a system of economic totalitarianism treats the industrious and the idle, the able and the stupid, as if they were alike—which is contrary to the laws of justice. Another of these reasons is the belief that only a society which, by and large, is economically free can be an orderly society; for the orderly society is one in which every class and interest fulfills the functions for which it is best suited, and without economic freedom a class of economic autocrats can domineer over all the other elements in society. Yet one more reason is the belief that the value of a system may be judged by that system's fruits; and the free economies of modern times, particularly in the United States, have been economically fruitful.

"It will take some hammering to drive a coddling socialism into America," George Santayana wrote nearly forty years ago. Yes; and the proportion of professed socialists is smaller in the United States, indeed, than it was when Santayana wrote. The great American labor unions never have flirted long with economic collectivism, and the number of economic radicals among educated people is smaller in the United States than in most countries; while the American merchant and industrialist remain undismayed champions of economic competition and free enterprise. Yet it remains possible for a nation to lose economic freedom through a failure to understand the necessary conditions of such freedom, just as it is possible for a people to lose political freedom in a fit of absence of mind. Our first necessity, then, is to apprehend the theories which lie behind the reality of our free economy.

Danger of exaggerated economic slogans

Sometimes, indeed, vociferous American devotees of "American capitalism" and "the American standard of living" do more mischief than benefit to their own cause, generating more heat than light, and substituting facile slogan for a grasp of first principles. It is presumptuous to urge an American soldier, for instance, to die for his American standard of living; and an American soldier would have to be very stupid to do anything of the sort. If by "standard of living" is meant simply the material goods and services which people happen to enjoy, it is folly to die for this; since the only way to enjoy a standard of *living* is to live. And it would be still more foolish to die for someone else's standard of living. To die for religion, justice, order, freedom, honor, or the lives of other people usually is a noble act. But to die for one's own creature-comforts, or for someone else's creature-comforts, always is a very ridiculous act. It is an insult to an American soldier to ask him to die for a new automobile or an apple pie; but it is a compliment to an American soldier to ask him to die for the ashes of his fathers and the temples of his God.

Economic production a means to ends

So we ought not to exaggerate the importance of our economic arguments or of our American economy. In many ways, the free economy of the United States is a good thing in itself; yet it is not the whole of life. No economy, however productive materially, could be a good thing if it were founded upon injustice, disorder, slavery, and dishonor. The slave-labor camps of the Soviet Union are economically efficient, after a fashion —but only because they take no reckoning of human lives or moral principles. Thus our American economy, though good in itself, is important not merely for its own sake: its real importance is the contribution it makes to our justice and order and freedom, our ability to live in dignity as truly human persons. Our "standard of living," though often enjoyable in itself, is not the be-all and end-all of life. Economic production is merely the means to certain ends. One of those ends is the satisfaction of men's material wants. And there are other ends served by this means of economic production: the satisfaction of certain profound desires in human nature, such as the desire for fruitful work and sufficient leisure and hopeful competition, for one; and the maintenance of a decent society, for another.

Now in the economic realm, what is the American cause? It seems to be the defense of an economic system which allows men and women to make their own principal choices in life; which reinforces political liberty; which adequately supplies the necessities of life; which recognizes and guides beneficently the deep-seated human longing for competition and mensurable accomplishment. What we call the "free economy" does these things.

Marx and "capitalism"

Karl Marx, the chief exponent of modern socialism, popularized both the term "capitalism" and the term "communism." Marx thought that all of life is merely an exercise in economics: he would have cast religion aside altogether, and would have made literature and the arts merely the slaves of politico-economic movements, and would have sacrificed freedom, gladly, to his idol of economic equality. His latter-day disciples, the Communists of the Soviet Union and their allies, still maintain these radical doctrines in all their rigor. "Communism," in theory, is the ownership of all property, collectively, by "the workers"; and the distribution of all goods and services according to need—so far as possible, on terms of exact equality—regardless of individual differences and private rights. (In practice, modern applied Communism has not worked out this way at all; but that is another matter.) Material production is the whole end and aim of a Communist society: material goods are all that make life worth living, in the eyes of the thoroughgoing Communist; and for the thoroughgoing Communist, there can be no life except the fleeting life which we experience here and now, on this earth.

Against this Communist ideal, Marx set an economic society which he called "capitalism": the economic system that prevailed in his own day. Marx hated many things; but most of all he hated capitalism and its works. By "capitalism," he meant an economic system in which the means of production is owned by private persons. Marx believed that such a system defrauded the workers of their just due, caused wars, and led inevitably to social decay. Once capitalism was thoroughly extirpated, Marx argued, all men would be free. To attain this perfect society of Communism, Marx predicted, the working classes, the "proletariat," would revolt fiercely against their capitalist masters, seize the means of production,

establish a proletarian dictatorship, turn the world upside down, and eventually watch the state wither away
until everyone might enjoy the fruits of economic production without masters or duties. And this would be the
end of history; thereafter, mankind would live forever in
a changeless state of satisfaction.

Meaning of Communism

To most Americans, substantially content with their
own country's social and economic order, the vision of
Marx seems a ludicrous caricature of the modern economy and a hopelessly fantastic grasping after what never
can be. Yet Marx's writings have succeeded, in combination with other factors, in turning half the world inside
out. Uniting with the discontent which always is present
in any society, and with disturbances in modern society
that accompany the spread of the industrial revolution
and the decay of old ways of life, Marxism became a
political religion, an ideology, conquering half of Europe
and three-fourths of Asia, and influencing opinion nearly
everywhere else, quite as speedily as Mohammedanism
spread across Asia and Africa twelve centuries ago.

There is not space here to refute the doctrines of
Marxism in detail; and, besides, most Marxists are not
affected by mere logical argument. "To consider whether
Marx was 'right' or 'wrong'; to dredge Volumes I and III
of *Capital* for inconsistencies or logical flaws, to 'refute'
the Marxian system," Professor Alexander Gray writes,
"is, in the last resort, sheer waste of time; for when we
consort with Marx we are no longer in the world of reason

or logic. He saw visions—clear visions of the passing of all things, much more nebulous visions of how all things may be made new. And his visions, or some of them, awoke a responsive chord in the hearts of many men." It is also not of much use to inquire whether Soviet Communism is "true Marxism"; for "true Marxism" never can be attained so long as human beings remain human. Soviet Communism is simply what any society falls into when it makes the terrible experiment of overthrowing established justice and order and freedom in the pursuit of that will-o'-the-wisp called Communism.

Adam Smith

So all we shall try to do in this chapter is to state quite simply the principles which lie behind the free economy that we know in America. These are principles which thinking men have understood, in part at least, for a great many centuries. They were expressed afresh, and more systematically than before, near the close of the eighteenth century, most notably by a Scottish professor of moral philosophy, Adam Smith. The teachings of Adam Smith and other British and French political economists were widely read and applied by the American generation which established the Republic. Although some of these doctrines of the eighteenth- and nineteenth-century economists have been modified by subsequent speculation and experience, for the most part the case for a free economy remains as Smith put it. The wealth of nations, Smith wrote, depends upon an economy in which there are free competition, sufficient reward for private industry and private saving, and reliance upon the ordinary motives to ordinary integrity. Such a society, such an economy, is guided by an "invisible hand": the natural law of economic existence which rules that every man, though laboring for his own benefit, actually increases the common good through his private labors. It is a powerful case that Smith puts.

Definition of capital

We may call this system of free enterprise "capitalism," if we like, though that Marxist word does not really mean very much. "Capital" is simply those goods—tools, machines, buildings, ships, trains, and the like—which are used to produce other goods. Any civilized society, therefore, is "capitalistic," since capital goods always are required to produce consumer goods. A communistic society requires capital quite as much as a "capitalistic" society does. But what Marx meant by "capitalism" is the ownership of capital by private persons. In that sense, America undoubtedly is a capitalistic country: nowhere else in the world, in any age, has the ownership of capital been as widespread as it is today, directly or indirectly, in the United States. And the defense of this economy is an important part of the American cause.

Idea of competition

At the heart of the theory of the free economy lies the idea of competition. Something in human nature seems to call for the possibility of a real victory in life—and the possibility of a real defeat. Life is enjoyable only because Hope exists: hope for success of one sort or another. And hope for success cannot exist without a corresponding dread of failure. In a very real sense, life is a battle; we never could be happy were it otherwise. Strong men enjoy struggling against obstacles; life without obstacles is boredom, just as life without purposeful work is infinitely dreary. Even were it possible—which it is not—for men and women to exist as the grown-up children of Marx's vision, spending their time idly in hunting and fishing and criticizing at dinner, men and women would be terribly bored by such an existence. To be rich without duties or challenges—to be the "idle rich" long denounced by the radical agitator—is to be unhappy all one's life. So human beings are content only when they are struggling against obstacles: and the form which that struggle ordinarily takes, we call competition.

Most of us enjoy competing against our neighbors, in one fashion or another; and, naturally, the instinct for competition is strongest in the more energetic and able men and women. Through competition, talents are developed and utilized which otherwise would be neglected; even the losers in the human competitive race profit from the existence of competition, because the abilities and the goods produced by the able in the competitive struggle benefit everyone in society. Now competition takes various forms; and if it is competition without any moral checks, it can be vicious. Competition of any sort ought to be governed by conscience and the rules of morality. Yet, by and large, competition is the means through which most improvement of society is accomplished: intellectual competition, and military competition, and economic competition. And economic competition, at least if it is influenced by moral principles, almost always does good to everyone in society. As Samuel Johnson said once, "A man is seldom more innocently occupied than when he is engaged in making money." This economic competition is essential to a free economy.

Motives to integrity

"Ordinary integrity," Edmund Burke wrote, "must be secured by the ordinary motives to integrity." Men and women are industrious, thrifty, honest, and ingenious, in economic life, only when they expect to gain certain rewards for being industrious, thrifty, honest, and ingenious. Some few human beings, in any age, work simply out of altruism, desire to benefit their fellows; but the vast majority work principally out of self-interest, to benefit themselves and their families. There is nothing wrong with this state of affairs; it is merely a condition of ordinary human nature. Competition puts a premium on industry, thrift, honesty, and ingeniousness, for the slothful, the spendthrift, the known cheats, and the stupid fall behind in the economic contest of free enterprise. Yet even these latter share to some extent in the benefits of competition, since the abilities and the goods developed by their more successful neighbors are distributed to the whole of society. The more industry, thrift, honesty, and ingeniousness the world can encourage, the better off the whole world is. By following their own self-interest, the able men and women serve the public interest. And the habits and skills which intelligent competition stimulates tend to improve, by example, even the less able members of society; while the rewards of successful competition, in terms of prestige and material gain, serve as the ordinary motives to ordinary integrity. Industry, thrift, honesty, and ingeniousness deserve concrete rewards. A competitive economy provides those rewards.

Compulsion as a substitute

If a society is deprived of competition, it is forced to rely either upon altruism, the unselfish efforts of men and women who work without reward; or upon compulsion, force employed to make people work without reward. Now the number of utterly unselfish men and women always is very small—insufficient to provide for the wants of the mass of society. And the use of compulsion to enforce work and a semblance of industry, thrift, honesty, and ingeniousness is slavery—incompatible with a free society and the concept of the dignity of man. Therefore a society without economic competition either falls into a dismal decay, because there are not enough unselfish people to do the world's work; or else it falls into slavery, the degradation of human nature and civilization. It has been said that there are two ways to persuade a donkey to carry his load; to show him a carrot, or to show him a stick. Mankind carries the load of the world's work for one of two reasons: either because of the incentive of ordinary rewards for ordinary integrity, the carrot; or else because of the hard punishment of failure, the stick. It is much more pleasant to live in a society with the promise of carrots than in a society with the threat of sticks. When the Russians swept away economic competition and abolished all the old motives to ordinary integrity, they found themselves compelled to resort to severe punishments in order to get work done at all. The slave-labor camps of the Soviet Union, the industrial spies and informers, the rigid production-quotas for factories and individuals, the enslavement of a whole nation, are the manifest consequences of abolishing competition.

And free labor generally is much more effectual than servile labor. When men and women work for their own improvement, they work with the best that is in them; but when they work only because of fear of the stick, they do as little as possible. Economically and morally, a competitive system is nothing to be ashamed of. On the contrary, it provides for human wants, and respects human freedom, far better than can any vague scheme of reliance solely upon altruism, or any system of forced labor. In essence, it is not competition which is ruthless; rather, it is the lack of competition that makes a society ruthless; because in a competitive economy people work voluntarily for decent rewards, while in a non-competitive economy a few harsh masters employ the stick to get the world's work done.

Economic Principle: The Free Economy

Charity and competition

A competitive society in which sound moral principles prevail is not a selfish or ruthless society. Through charity, such a society provides for the needs of those who, because of one handicap or another, cannot provide for themselves in the economic contest. The successful, in such a society, are taught by moral precepts that it is their moral duty to give voluntarily to their neighbors who stand in need of aid. Competition does not rule out love and pity. In a genuinely competitive society, most such acts of charity are private and local, the work of individuals and voluntary organizations, though in emergencies and in cases beyond the scope of private action the government takes a hand. Enlightened competition does not mean "dog eat dog." Successful competition makes possible successful charity: for the increased productivity of a competitive free economy gives society a surplus of goods and services with which to relieve the poor, the infirm, the handicapped, the old, and the young.

A free economy is one in which men and women can make their own choices. They can choose the kind of work they want to do, and where they want to do it. They can buy what they choose, and abstain from what they choose. They can work when they like, within limits, and rest when they like. They can change occupations and employers and their material circumstances much as they like. These are great benefits: they help to satisfy the fundamental human longing for self-reliance. They make men and women free.

Servile economy

But an economy without competition is a system in which men and women are allowed almost no free choices. It is a regimented, a servile, economy. In such a system, everything must be totally planned. A small body of persons, who are the real masters of society under such circumstances—called commissars, or planners, or what you will—must determine what is to be produced, and who is to receive it, and who shall do what work, and what people shall be paid, and where and how long they shall work, and how they shall be punished if they do not work. Even questions of taste and style must be fixed by a bureau under such a regime. Such a system keeps men and women in perpetual childhood, their wants provided for by central authority, and their choices, in proportion, made for them by central authority. Human life under such conditions discourages the full development of mind and character. A great critic of literature, George Saintsbury, expressed with loathing the general curse of such a society: "Put away all thought of the crime and agony which would have to be gone through in order to bring about the Socialist Utopia; get it somehow brought about by fairy agency; could there, even then, be anything more loathsome than one wide waste of proletariat-Cocqcigrue comfort; everybody as good as the President; everybody as 'well educated' as everybody else; everybody stationed, rationed, regulated by some kind of abstract 'State'—as equal, and really as free, as pigs in a sty, and not much better deserving the name of man, or the manly chances of position, possession, genius, ancestry, and all that differentiates us from the brutes?"

The collectivistic economy necessarily abolishes every sort of freedom: for men and women must eat; and if some central authority is able to tell them whether or not they shall eat, and how much, and under what circumstances, they are the slaves of that central authority, even though that totalitarian economic system may call itself "democratic." Compulsory labor under the direction of powerful administrators is the most conspicuous feature of any functioning regimented economy. The man who fails to obey, or to produce his quota, is denounced as a "saboteur," and every stimulus to private initiative and ingenuity is discouraged. In exchange for a fancied economic security—in exchange for a promise from the state to supply all the necessities of life—half the world has given up its economic freedom. But this is a devil's bargain: for with economic freedom, political freedom and private rights also vanish. And the totalitarian state does not fulfill its part of the bargain, since once the old motives to industry and thrift and honesty and ingenuity have been swept away, the driving force behind a country's system of economic production is terribly weakened; production declines and invention languishes; even the ferocious powers of compulsion exercised by the totalitarian state seldom compensate for the decline of private integrity and competition. In the modern industrial world, it really is not possible to buy economic security at the price of liberty. It is possible only to surrender freedom in exchange for total planning —which relieves most people of the necessity for making their own choices in life, but also relieves them of their prosperity and their birthright as human beings.

Social justice, true and false

So the free economy, characterized by liberty of choice, private ownership of capital, and competition, is a bulwark of all freedom. It also is a bulwark of justice. Justice, we ought not to forget, means "to each his own" —to each man the things which suit his own nature. Zealots for economic collectivism talk a great deal about "social justice"—by which they mean that all people ought to have an equal share in the world's goods. Closely examined, however, their theories can produce only social injustice; for once applied, those theories deprive men and women of the rewards that belong to their nature. Even Karl Marx knew that Communism must treat unfairly—in any established meaning of the word "fairness"—the abler and more talented people. "In order to establish equality," Marx wrote in *Capital,* a century ago, "we must first establish inequality." By this he meant that the Communistic state will take away from the strong, the clever, the thrifty, the ingenious, the dependable—from all the people who have unusual abilities and savings—and will give their property and the product of their energies to the weak, the dull, the improvident, the routine-minded, the slack. For complete equality of condition in this world can be established only if a society is willing to penalize the better natures in order to benefit the less gifted natures. If we believe in the idea of justice which lies at the root of classical and Christian thought, such an undertaking would be not justice, but gross injustice; it would deny to most of the better men and women the things which belong to their nature—the rewards of private integrity.

Pure equality impossible

Nor is such a complete equality possible in any society. It has not come to pass in any of the modern Communistic states, for there the commissars and party leaders enjoy power and material rewards immensely greater than the average. Leadership, whether it is good or bad leadership, always will exact rewards. It is possible, through revolution or unjust laws, to abolish the property-rights and the incomes of the present possessors of capital and the present leaders of society. But it is not possible to abolish leadership and the necessary rewards of leadership. All that a Communist revolution accomplishes, in reality, is to supplant the old leadership by a host of squalid oligarchs spewed up by the violence of the revolution; and these new political and economic masters are far harder and less charitable than the old.

Totalist economy and disorder

A regimented economy is unjust, then; and also it is disorderly. For order means that a society recognizes its natural leaders, in their rightful functions: its principled statesmen, its sincere clergy, its learned scholars, its energetic men of business, its skilled craftsmen; it gives

109

all these, and all other orders in society, their due. But the collectivistic economy abolishes all these distinctions and functions, substituting for the healthy variety of a free economy a new elite of bureaucrats and party agents, who usurp the functions and the rewards of all those beneficial orders. There remain in the totalitarian economy only two classes: the arrogant new elite of managers and planners, and the faceless crowd of the "proletariat," subservient to the demands of the total state. Through the employment of force and surveillance, such a collectivistic state may keep the peace; but it is hopelessly disorderly in the sense that it has repudiated the principles of free choice and natural leadership.

It is not the American mission to compel or persuade all the world to copy "American capitalism." If the American people believe in free choice at home, they must support the principle of free choice among nations. America has no moral imperative, for instance, to abolish the communal system of land-cultivation prevalent in Java, or to make the Swiss give up their system of state-owned railways. Every nation must choose its own institutions. But Americans do have the right, and the duty, to defend their own free economy, with all its benefits, against collectivistic attack or subversion: to defend their economy in the interest of freedom and justice and order and prosperity. And Americans do have the right to assist other countries in which a free economy is menaced by the designs of the economic collectivists; for even the vigorous American economy would have difficulty surviving in a world dominated by totalitarian states. Whatever its shortcomings, the American system of free enterprise has given our nation a prosperity very rare in any age; and it is infinitely freer and juster and more orderly than any collectivistic scheme of total regulation.

CHAPTER 8

Economic Principle: American Economic Accomplishment

American standard of living

The greatness and contentment of a nation are not measured merely by that nation's wealth. Compared with any modern state, Athens in the fifth century before Christ was extremely poor; but the world has not seen since such intellectual brilliance as then resided in Athens. One of the most remote and thinly-populated of modern countries, Iceland, appears to be at once among the most nearly contented and the most highly cultured of nations; while some of the states with the larger national incomes also have the higher rates of suicide and crime. So although American prosperity is something for which Americans ought to be thankful, nevertheless they ought not to rest their whole case, when they defend the American cause, upon the evidences of American wealth. Braggart nations, like braggart men, generally are disliked; and smugness is a dangerous mood for any country, no matter how great its natural resources may be.

Yet, this said, the United States undeniably is a great economic success. Part of this success results from our natural resources; part from our size as a nation, which gives us one of the largest free-trade areas in the world; and part—probably the most important part—from the economic and political and moral principles by which we govern ourselves. The annual income of the average American family now is more than four thousand dollars, and the purchasing-power of that income is greater than any people ever have had before in all history. As the "standard of living" is usually measured, Americans live better than any other people; only a few states, notably Sweden, Switzerland, Canada, and Australia, even approach our scale of prosperity. Whether or not they always use their wealth wisely, at least Americans have the power to enjoy standards of diet, housing, and physical comfort previously unknown to mankind.

Concentration of wealth

And this wealth is very widely and equitably distributed. In 1956, wages and salaries comprised nearly two-thirds of the nation's total income of three hundred and forty billion dollars; if one adds to this the incomes of farmers, professional people, and small shopkeepers, it becomes clear that we have no great concentration of wealth and income in any class of "capitalists" in the United States. A generation ago, certain radical agitators invented the slogan that "five per cent of the people own ninety-five per cent of the wealth in the United States." This slogan was, and is, a baseless fabrication.

Never before, in any civilized society, has there been a greater equality of incomes than there is now in America. According to some economists, indeed, the trouble lies the other way: it is possible that we do not reward well enough the "upper classes," the more energetic and thrifty people among us. The number of millionaires has decreased greatly in the United States since 1929; while the number of people with merely comfortable incomes has increased greatly. Even in the Russian Communist system, the leaders in government and industry receive larger rewards, in proportion to the total national income, than do their counterparts in the American system. The disproportion between the income of the successful commissar and the income of the average Soviet worker is much greater than the difference between the income of the successful American businessman and the average American worker.

Millions of "capitalists"

The real income of Americans continues to rise steadily, and is reflected in private savings and in our "people's capitalism," through which more and more Americans are coming to own a share in American industry. Most of our "capitalists" are people of moderate means, who own stocks or bonds or insurance-policies invested in large commercial and industrial corporations; millions of our private investors are men and women who work with their hands. American labor unions, indeed, now are "capitalists" in their own right, since the gigantic pension-funds and reserves of the unions usually are invested in the stocks and bonds of "private" corporations. One index of our general prosperity and stability, extending to every order in American society, is the steady increase in the number of houses privately owned by their occupants; among the great states, America stands first in the world in family ownership of homes. Although local, state, and federal governments have undertaken large-scale projects of slum-clearance and low-rent public housing, these developments are much more modest, in proportion to the total population, than they are in much of Europe; and the reason for this is that most American families are able, and willing, to pay for their own houses.

American material achievements

In education, primary, secondary, and advanced, Americans spend more per capita than any other people; we have far more students, per head of population, enrolled in institutions of higher learning than has any other country. In medical treatment and hospitalization, we are better off than any other nation; voluntary private health-insurance organizations, growing rapidly in every American state, provide the American alternative to socialized medicine. We have reduced the worries of old age by elaborate systems of pensions and insurance, both private and public. And our economy seems remarkably stable, as national economies go: we have had no stock-market "crash" since 1929, and our periods of recession or temporary unemployment are brief and moderate. No one need starve in America. We take this fact so much for granted that we tend to forget what a remarkable fact it is. Until well into the nineteenth century, throughout the world, on the contrary, starvation was taken for granted: it was thought inevitable that, from time to time, thousands or even millions of men and women and children must starve in times of famine or industrial disorder. In much of Asia and Africa and South America and even Europe, occasional starvation still is taken for granted. And it is worth noting that mass-starvation continues to take place in the principal Communist nations, Russia and China.

American economic experience refutes Marx

Now this prosperity of our free ecenomy would have confounded Karl Marx. For Marx predicted that a dreadful decay of the "capitalistic" system was inevitable; the rich would grow steadily richer, and the poor poorer; capitalistic imperialism would loot and oppress the whole world; the working classes would be ground into misery, and the ownership of property, increasingly, would be concentrated in the hands of a few unscrupulous people of immense means. Yet in the United States, the most "capitalistic" of great countries, quite the opposite has taken place. Communism would come first to the most advanced industrial nations, he prophesied; while on the contrary, Communism has triumphed in those nations industrially retarded—Russia, China, and the small countries of Eastern Europe. Something was very wrong with Marx's analysis of economics, and

American economic accomplishment is a great flourishing disproof of Marxist theories.

Technology and freedom

Our American prosperity is not simply an accident. Our technology, our industrial ingenuity, has much to do with our economic success, of course; but that technology, in considerable part, is itself the product of a free economy. For a free economy offers great material rewards to invention, efficiency, and shrewd management. Competition tends to eliminate the inefficient and obsolete, and to put a premium upon new methods and discoveries. An industrialist or a merchant is responsible for his own blunders, and is entitled to the profits of his ability, under a system of free enterprise; no dead hand of state regulation lies heavy upon the conduct of the economy. Business is left to businessmen, as it ought to be, except for a minimum of regulation in the interest of fair play; and technology is left to the technicians and scientists. A man works best when he works freely, for his own advantage. His inventions and increases of capital may be initially for his own benefit, but in the long run they benefit all society.

Free enterprise and leisure

Marx was wrong: free enterprise does not lead to servitude and poverty for the masses. By liberating energies, a free economy encourages every man to do his best. It is free enterprise, indeed, that has abolished slavery in the Western world. Slavery exists either when many people will not work hard enough or long enough except under compulsion, or when the only way to provide that leisure essential to society seems to be to make some people work hard and long in order that a minority may have leisure for thought and leadership. The classical world saw no alternative to slavery; the Old South saw no alternative to slavery. But whatever the industrial age of competition and free enterprise has done or failed to do, certainly it has emancipated the mass of men and women from involuntary labor. Until the triumph of modern industry—which went hand in hand with the triumph of a free economy—it was possible to obtain leisure only by living upon the labor of others, or by living in poverty, forgoing creature comforts in the interest of the contemplative life. But today, and especially in America, it is possible for everyone to have relatively abundant leisure: this is the work of industrial efficiency and a free economy.

Nowadays most Americans work only forty hours a week—a vast improvement over the conditions of a century past. There is talk even of a four-day week. For the mass of people, such a quantity of free time is a novelty, so that some spend their free hours only in idleness, which is boring. But though we have not yet solved the problems created by widespread leisure, at any rate we have refuted the Marxist prediction that men under "capitalism" would have to work increasingly hard for diminished pay. We have increased the leisure of people who work with their hands, indeed, more greatly than we have increased the leisure of people who work with their minds. Every element in our society has shared in the benefits of our prosperity, with the possible exceptions of the people of established wealth, the clergy, the professors of arts and sciences, and some of the small farmers. Even our farmers, despite frequent complaints, are better off economically than they used to be, most of them; it is only relatively that they have not kept up, in recent years, with the prosperity of their city cousins. Farm income, in short, has increased, but has not increased so much as has the income of people in manufacturing and the service industries; yet the farmer, in terms of work and comfort, now has a much easier life than had his father or grandfather.

No depressed classes

We have no arbitrarily depressed class in America. The radical critic of American institutions takes pleasure in denouncing the condition of Negroes in the United States. Yet when one looks at their actual circumstances, one finds the soundest proofs of a steady advance in their economic and social advantages. In the past two decades especially, the incomes and living-standards of American Negroes have swept rapidly upward. From a condition of rural poverty and servitude, denied civil rights, less than a century ago, the American Negro has made his way to comparative prosperity, North and South; more and more, he approaches economic equality with white Americans. And with his economic gains have come social gains. As he has grown wealthier, so he has

tended to acquire political and social privileges; for social equality generally follows upon economic equality.
Sound progress, particularly in economic life, cannot be
made overnight, or merely by passing laws; it has to
come out of a solid foundation of gradual achievement.
The remarkable fact is not that the Negro, less than a
century away from abject slavery, is poorer than his
white neighbor, on the average: what is truly remarkable is the extent to which this minority has shared in
the national progress. American treatment of the Negro,
economic and social and political, will more than bear
comparison with the treatment of racial minorities anywhere else in the world; the Russian Communists, whose
way with minorities often is extirpation, are hypocritical
in their denunciations of our record.

Prosperity no guarantee of happiness

Economic prosperity cannot guarantee human happiness. Happiness, for that matter, is very difficult to define. Who is happier, J. F. Stephen asks in his book
Liberty, Equality, Fraternity: "a very stupid prosperous
farmer who dies of old age after a life of perfect health,
or an accomplished delicate woman of passionate sensi-
bility and brilliant genius, who dies worn out before her
youth is passed, after an alternation of rapturous happiness with agonies of distress?" And, Stephen says, this is
like "asking the distance from one o'clock to London
Bridge"; one man's happiness is another man's pain.
Mankind never is perfectly content either with work or

with leisure; the rich are not free from care; and prosperous nations still have their problems. So Americans are imprudent if they argue that American prosperity demonstrates the superiority of all American institutions. It is entirely possible for a Portuguese peasant or an Austrian monk to be happier than an American businessman, though it is not possible for him to be richer. When the American talks of freedom to the people of India, he tends to fall into the error of identifying freedom with material prosperity. But for the Indian who knows his native traditions, "freedom" means the absence of worldly desire, and thus the American merely puzzles him; besides, it is improbable that India ever can be one-third so prosperous as the United States; so boasts of American wealth may merely excite envy. We ought not to make too much of the economic argument when we are defending the American cause.

So far as material achievement can satisfy human longings, nevertheless, we Americans have gone further than have any other people; and we have diffused our prosperity more widely throughout our nation. To leaf through the annual *Statistical Abstract of the United States* is to obtain overwhelming proof of our economy's success. And anyone who has travelled a little in America sees the evidences of a tremendous material accomplishment on every hand—a prosperity expressed in better houses, better food, new automobiles, great schools and public buildings, splendid highways, a multitude of popular luxuries. In the face of all this evidence, how can the Communists and other revolutionary doctrinaires continue to argue that America is a land of capitalistic oppression and failure?

Misrepresentations of Communists

The answer is simple enough: the Communist and his fellows really are not interested in facts, or in economic prosperity. They profess to be eager to improve the material condition of the masses; in theory, economic improvement is the whole purpose of life, so far as they are concerned; but in reality the twentieth-century Communists and other totalitarians are perfectly indifferent to sober economic achievement or to human suffering. In actuality, they want revolution for its own sake, not revolution to improve society; they want power for its own sake, not power to achieve good. They talk of the "downtrodden proletariat" because that sort of talk tends to rouse resentments in many quarters, to prepare the ground for revolution, to awake a sense of injustice where often no injustice exists, to stimulate expectations which never can be realized. They hope, too, by this sort of talk, to weaken the will to resist among the defenders of true justice and order and freedom; they hope to give Americans and others a case of bad conscience, which will render them feeble when confronted by determined Communist demands. But when the Communists and other totalitarians succeed in achieving power, they treat the "oppressed masses" with thoroughgoing contempt and brutality. The Soviet domination of Hungary is sufficient illustration. The Hungarian economy is bled white to provide goods for the Communist masters of Russia; and when Hungarian workingmen protest, they are shot down as "Fascists," "reactionaries," and "capitalists." In sober fact, the hardest "capitalistic" master of nineteenth-century industry was a model of charity and compassion by the side of the average commissar.

The intelligent Communist—excluding here those Communists and fellow-travellers who are simply stupid or confusedly sentimental—is a man obsessed by two passions, envy and the lust for power. He desires to tear down whatever is old and venerable in civilized life, and to build upon the ruins his own gloomy fortress of absolute tyranny. To this end, he is willing—sworn, indeed—to use every tool he can: to cheat and to lie. No matter how successful the American economy may be, therefore, he will denounce it as a failure. Communism is his religion; subversion is his creed. He does not really seek a tranquil and prosperous society; all he desires is the triumph of his party. It is impossible to persuade the thoroughgoing Communist of the benefits of American economic life, because his whole interest lies in destroying that life. One might as well try to convince a wolf of the pleasures of life in the sheepfold.

Yet the unreasonableness of the Communist does not make the American cause hopeless. For most people, in any country, never become hardened members of the Communist party. The average man, anywhere, is not inevitably envious and power-hungry. The very unreasonableness of Communism, indeed, is an asset to the

American cause; for man naturally is a rational being, and can be convinced by evidence and experience. In much of the world, populations under Communist domination already are disillusioned with Communist slogans. If Americans can put their case for order and justice and freedom clearly and reasonably, they may hope to undo the unreason of Communism; and surely they can be confident of checking subversion at home. The hardened Communist is a man possessed by a devil, as some might put it; or a man afflicted by a pathological state of mind, as others might say. Only a failure of nerve on the part of the defenders of order and justice and freedom, only a misunderstanding of their own first principles by the friends of the American cause, can allow the fanaticism of Communism to triumph over right reason.

American economy contrasted with totalist economy

American society is imperfect; but all human societies are imperfect in some degree. The American economy has its faults; but they are faults which may be modified. The faults of Communism are so profound that they cannot be ameliorated. A free economy, because of its opportunities for choice and competition, has always within it the possibilities of improvement; it does not repress the reformer. But a totalitarian economy, hostile to any sort of criticism, founded on envy and terror, cannot amend its ways without ceasing to be; it leaves no room for prudent reformation. When something in a free economy goes wrong, there is temporary trouble, but the variety of talents and the elasticity of the economic structure make mending fairly easy. When, however, something in a totalitarian economy goes wrong, there is general and serious suffering, because the master-plan of the regimented economy is inelastic and arbitrary. The free economy, in such conditions, penalizes only a few men by loss of profit, or resort to bankruptcy. But when the totalitarian economy is brought to account for its mistakes, it seeks scapegoats: and the concentration camp substitutes for the bankruptcy-court.

American economic problems

It will not do for us to be complacent about our American economy. We have many grave problems. We need to humanize mass-production, and to restore craftsmanship and personal accomplishment to work, and to teach ourselves how to make our leisure something better than boredom. We need to infuse into modern industrial life a sense of community and purpose and hope and deep-rooted security. We need more genuinely educated businessmen and more genuinely responsible labor-union leaders. We need decentralization of industry and more penetrating regard for the claims of rural life.

But none of these problems can be solved by economic collectivism. Communism, the sham of "total economic planning," is death to prosperity, as it is fatal to freedom. It abolishes the ordinary motives to ordinary integrity; for enlightened self-interest, it substitutes a new and more thorough slavery. It rewards intrigue and betrayal; it punishes honesty and diligence and charity. In the

125

name of making all men equal, it makes all men servile. Its claims run counter to the deepest instincts of human nature. What is unnatural never can make men happy. Communism abolishes the opportunities for personal advancement and enduring accomplishment which our economic system has made available to all people willing to work. In upholding a free economy, Americans are upholding the material fabric of an elevated civilization.

CHAPTER 9

The Communist Claims

In every age there is much human discontent; and in nearly every age there arises some revolutionary movement which takes advantage of that discontent. In our own time, the particular revolutionary radicalism which exploits our present discontents is called Communism.

Discontent produced by confusion

We would be smug and silly to deny that there are reasons for discontent with modern life. It is not ordinarily poverty which creates discontent, for the great majority of men usually have been poor and yet reasonably contented with their lot; and some of the least wealthy nations nowadays are the most tranquil. It is not lack of wealth which produces modern discontent and opens the gates to the Communists. There are almost no Communists in Ireland, one of the poorest countries of the Western world. There are many Communists in France, a relatively prosperous and "developed" country. What really creates discontent in the modern age, as in all ages, is confusion and uncertainty. Men turn to radical doctrines not when they are poor, but when they are emotionally and intellectually distraught. When faith in their ancient religion is shaken; when old rulers and old forms of government disappear; when profound economic changes alter their modes of livelihood; when the expectation of private and public change becomes greater than the expectation of private and public continuity; when even the family seems imperilled; when men can no longer live as their fathers lived before them, but wander bewildered in new ways—then the radical agitator, of one persuasion or another, has a fertile field to cultivate. Men do not often rebel against mere privation, but they frequently revolt against the confusion of their society. And usually their rebellion only makes that confusion worse confounded.

Thus it is the giddy pace of change in the modern world which has generated our modern discontents. So far as technology is concerned, there has been more change in the past two centuries than in the whole preceding three thousand years; and in some lands, this change of technology, which we usually call the "industrial revolution," has been compressed into a single generation of the twentieth century. Roughly parallel with these revolutionary technological changes in civilization have come social and intellectual changes equally catastrophic, such as the decay of established religious and moral beliefs, the malfunctioning of old political institutions, and an immense increase in population over much of the world. It is no wonder that men and women have found it difficult to adjust themselves to this giddy change. But to turn the world upside down in resentment at the world's confusion is no remedy.

We can discern in history other such ages of confusion produced by rapid change, such as the fifth century before Christ in Greece, and the first century before Christ in Rome. In those times, too, confusion led to revolution, war, and tyranny. In our own century, the revolutions of our times have been produced by this confused protest at the rapidity of change. Men embrace fantastic proposals when they are bewildered and insecure. The Nazis came to power in Germany, the most prosperous and energetic and best-schooled of European nations, upon the wave of this confused discontent. The Communists of Russia took advantage of the Russian defeat in the First World War to impose themselves upon that immense country. The Communists in China rose upon the ruin of the ancient Chinese civilization. The Communists of central Europe triumphed only because—aside from the support of Russian armies—Europe was utterly bewildered in the aftermath of the Second World War. When men have lost their accustomed beliefs and their established ways of life—whether they are rich or poor—they tend to seek some political religion, some fanaticism which promises them peace of body and mind. Knowing this ancient weakness in human nature, in the twentieth century the Communists have been able to make themselves masters of a great part of the world. They have flourished by the indecision and groping discontent of the majority of men.

129

Communism an ideology

So Communism is not truly a reasoned social philosophy, but instead what is properly called an "ideology," a fanatic political creed that promises to its disciples what no simple political or economic alteration really can accomplish. It is, as Burke said of Jacobinism in the French Revolution, "an armed doctrine." It holds forth to the confused and discontented the Utopia of a classless society, in which all material wants will be supplied without personal responsibility, and in which change will have been abolished. What it promises is a caricature of the Christian vision of Heaven. It is Heaven upon Earth, but with God eliminated. Philosophically and historically speaking, the Communist Utopian is mad. But that fact does not diminish his appeal to a great many people. In revolutionary times, as Alexis de Tocqueville writes, madness may be an advantage, leading to temporary success. The Communists promise what neither they nor anyone else can perform: that is, they promise to make human nature and society perfect by changing laws and social institutions. Their Utopia must always remain Nowhere-Land. Some apologists for Communism, embarrassed by the Russian example, argue that Russian Communism is not "true" Communism. This apology is correct in one sense only: that "true" Communism is impossible to establish in Russia or anywhere else. For "true" Communism is hopelessly impractical, running contrary to everything we know about human nature and society. Russian Communism is as close to "true" Communism as any state can come and still maintain a semblance of law and order and efficiency.

Pure Communism impossible

Communism is an illusion: in its "true" or "pure" form, it never can be established among men. Yet it is entirely possible, as the modern world knows to its cost, for persons calling themselves Communists to seize power, establish "Soviet Republics," and destroy order and justice and freedom and the finest works of civilization. What these triumphant Communists bring to a nation is not the promised Heaven upon Earth—which is impossible —but a very real Hell upon Earth. They can erect, and perhaps maintain indefinitely, a tyrannical regime which they describe as "Socialist," and which, they declare, is progressing toward "Communism." This "progress" usually consists of the extirpation of all opposition and the complete physical and intellectual subjugation of the people upon whom they have imposed their iron regime. Pure Communism is a delusion; but Soviet power is a grim reality.

Communists not reasonable men

So it is important to understand what manner of men the Communists are, and what doctrines they profess, and what arguments they employ to make converts, and particularly what accusations they make against the United States. As Professor Gerhart Niemeyer writes in his recent book *An Inquiry into Soviet Mentality*, these Communist doctrines and arguments and accusations

131

and tactics often are inconsistent, and often even the Communists themselves know them to be false. But the Communists are not seeking truth; they are seeking power. They are not even seeking, primarily, to fulfill the prophecies of Karl Marx. What the Communists are after is the total destruction of existing civilization, so that they can build upon the ruins their own totalist political structure. They are playing the great fierce game of power, in which the stakes are innumerable human lives, and in which the prizes are total domination of all aspects of human existence. Therefore the Communists do not concern themselves with whether their arguments and their methods are "reasonable" or "humane." As Dr. Niemeyer observes,

If there ever was a sense in which Marx' political objective—given certain premises—could be considered reasonable, the Communists' present political end cannot be called reasonable on any premise. It is the end of imposing upon the vast majority of mankind the ideas and the will of a small minority that has discovered new ways of manipulating human beings into subservience to totalitarian power. Even in their own minds the Communists do not see their rule as an implicit mandate of the majority of the people. They know that in coming to power they will disrupt, destroy, and distort most people's habits, preferences, and institutions. They are determined to achieve their goal in spite of immeasurable cost in human life, liberty, happiness, and dignity—a cost which, as their political organization proves, they calculate ahead of time. Communists are therefore required to argue their goal according to one set of terms and to pursue it according to a different set of terms: a situation not favorable for maintaining a proportionality between political ends and the costs of attaining them.*

Two types of Communist

Now what sort of person is the Communist, who is eager to "disrupt, destroy, and distort most people's habits, preferences, and institutions"? In general, there are two types of Communists:

(1) The naïve or sentimental Communist, who believes that something is hopelessly wrong with life as we know it and that Communism actually can provide the remedy for all the ills to which humanity is heir. Though such a person is a dangerous dreamer, he may be sincere. Wherever a Communist party comes actually to power, such sentimental Communists quickly are eliminated by their more realistic Communist colleagues, as "Utopians"—eliminated quite as ruthlessly as the "bourgeois obstructionists." But in countries like the United States, where a Communist regime never has attained power, it still is possible for some old-fashioned sentimental Communists to survive side by side with hardcore, realistic Communists. In such free states, the sentimental Communists have not yet had all their illusions dispelled by the behavior of a Communist clique established in power; and the free, "capitalistic" government protects such sentimental Communists, as it protects

* Gerhart Niemeyer, *An Inquiry into Soviet Mentality*, pp. 38-39.

everyone else, from the purges of the majority of Communists.

(2) The realistic, practical Communist, who may employ humanitarian phrases to win converts, but whose real aim is pure power. These "realistic" Communists, in every country, constitute the majority of members of the Communist party. They are not really concerned with improving the state of existing society, or with lessening the confusion and disorder which form the recruiting area for Communism. Having observed the actual functioning of Communist regimes, they know quite well that a Soviet Republic will not be humane or equalitarian or even efficient. These practical Communists have lost all their illusions, and yet they remain hard-core Communists. Some have gone too far in the Communist party to draw back now without great personal danger; others, still less scrupulous, are willing to sacrifice everything in our civilization—including their own honesty—for the gratified lust of absolute power in their own hands and the hands of their clique. Like O'Brien in Orwell's novel *1984*, they are compensated by the pleasure of "stamping forever on a human face."

If, then, Communists nowadays are either fools or evil men—for after the conduct of the Communist regimes in Russia and China and Hungary and elsewhere it is impossible for any reasonable man really to believe that Communism is the path to perfection—how is it that in many countries the Communists still make converts, and almost everywhere in the world they contrive to maintain an effective party organization, openly or underground, despite repeated disclosures of the inconsistency between Soviet professions and Soviet performance? The answer seems to be that Communism is greatly assisted by popular ignorance and popular envy.

Popular ignorance

Karl Marx expected that Communism would triumph first in the more advanced countries of Europe and North America, where industrialism was far advanced and where general literacy prevailed. In actuality, Communism has triumphed in the less industrialized and less literate states: countries bewildered by the rapid advance of modern technology and social institutions, to which changes they were unable to adjust in any orderly fashion. In the confusion that ensued, the Communists rose to power. The principal recent gains of the Communists have been in regions still less assimilated to twentieth-century life, and where still higher rates of illiteracy prevail. Thus the Communists have been dealing, for the greater part, with peoples substantially ignorant of Russian history and current affairs, and therefore given to accepting Soviet claims at face value. But even in their dealings with the principal Western powers, the Communists have been able to count upon a considerable degree of historical and political ignorance among the citizens of free nations. The docility with which most of our captured American soldiers in Korea accepted the doctrines of a handful of hastily-trained Chinese Communist indoctrinators suggests that real knowledge of Communist aims and performance, and real knowledge of the moral and social principles of our civilization, have not yet been acquired by the majority of Americans. Minds ignorant of principle easily are vanquished by ideology.

Popular envy

And where the abuse of ignorance will not suffice, the Communist resorts to the vice of envy. Envy, one of the most powerful and subtle of human emotions, is easily roused and difficult to repress. A man is not always aware of his own envy. Kierkegaard remarks somewhere that envy is unconscious and suppressed admiration. "Why should anyone else be more rich or famous or popular than I am?"—in all of us there stirs at least a little of this impulse.

So whenever an objection is raised to Communist purges, slave-labor camps, mass executions, and confiscations, the hardened Communist replies that the victims were "enemies of the people." The victims had property, and rank, and prestige, and power; and so they deserved their fate, for presuming to be better than you or I. When hundreds of thousands of Ukranian peasants were shipped away in boxcars to die in the Soviet arctic, the Communists attempted to justify this atrocity before the world as retribution upon agricultural profiteers. When uncounted thousands of Chinese were shot by Communist firing-squads after the Communist military victory in China, this was defended as the "liquidation of the selfish landlord class." (Most of the "landlords" put to death had held less than ten acres of land.)*

Yet these feeble and hypocritical excuses were accepted at face value by certain serious journals of opinion in America and Britain. It is easy, for a good many people, to conjure up a mental image of some Rich Bad Man who has to be shot because he stands in the way of the People's Progress. It is so hard for some people to confess to themselves that possibly the Communists are not kindly liberals who occasionally become a trifle impetuous. Envy, inverted admiration, is one of the most disastrous impulses of our modern age.

Canons of Communism

The abuse of ignorance and the rousing of envy are the hardened Communist's usual tools. But he also has a set of formal doctrines with which to impress the educated and the half-educated. The Communist deliberately cultivates obscurity in language in order to make his arguments sound "scientific" and profound. Yet the principal dogmas of the Communists can be set down quite simply and briefly. They are these:

* In a speech to Chinese Communist leaders in February, 1957, the Communist dictator of China, Mao Tse-Tung, admitted that eight hundred thousand people had been put to death by his regime during the four years after the nominal end of the Chinese Civil war—that is, between 1949 and 1954. Other estimates of the numbers slain by Communist policy run far into the millions. Mao said, "In dealing with enemies, it is necessary to use force. We in China also have used force to deal with enemies of the people. The total number of those who were liquidated by our security forces numbers 800,000."

(1) There is no God, and this life is the be-all and end-all. Therefore the material satisfaction of the masses is the only goal of life.

(2) All men and women ought to be equal in every way, especially in economic condition. "In order to establish equality," Marx wrote in *Capital*, "we must first establish inequality." He meant that the Communist dictatorship would take away from the strong, the intelligent, the industrious, the thrifty, and the inheritors of property, and give to those less favored by nature. "From each according to his ability, to each according to his need."

(3) This society of perfect equality is called Communism. To establish Communism, any means is justifiable. The destruction of the existing societies will be finally accomplished—after a period of subversion and gradual weakening—by violence. Then the "proletariat," the working classes, will establish a class dictatorship.*

(4) In time—Marx does not say how soon—this proletarian dictatorship will cease to be; the political state will wither away; and all mankind will live forever after in a classless, equalitarian, substantially changeless society, perfectly at peace.

(5) The only moral values are those of the proletariat, and the sole object of arts, literature, philosophy, and political activity is to wage the struggle of the proletariat

* Communist propagandists use the terms "communism" and "socialism" almost interchangeably. When indoctrinating American prisoners, they usually employed the word "socialism" to describe the Soviet system, this having a sound less disagreeable to American ears.

against the "bourgeoisie," the middle classes. Communism is an end in itself. It supersedes all religion, moral standards, and philosophy.

Measures to accomplish Communist revolution

To accomplish the triumph of Communism, Marx and Engels listed in the *Communist Manifesto* (1848) the program of action which all Communists must undertake. All private property in land was to be confiscated; a heavy progressive income tax was to be put into effect; the right of inheritance was to be abolished; the property of all opponents was to be confiscated; the state was to monopolize banking and credit; the state was to monopolize communication and transportation; the state was to acquire factories and other means of production, and to improve the soil through collective farming; "industrial armies" were to be formed, with conscription of everyone for manual labor; agriculture and manufacturing were to merge; the state was to monopolize education and unite schooling with industrial production.

Communist violence

Wherever the Communists have come to power, they have put into effect these measures for the abolition of established society. But their primary means for destroying the church, the family, the community, lawful governments, private associations, and private property has been violence. Communists never have come to power peacefully, and they never tolerate political opposition or permit free elections. Their favorite method for attaining power is through subversion: working their way into the government of a country gradually, through intimidation and deceit, under the pretext of being merely one of several parties in a democratic state; and then, when sufficiently entrenched, resorting to the murder or imprisonment of all their opponents, and—if necessary—calling in military support from some country already Communist-dominated, such as Russia or China. In any country, including Russia and China, the members of the Communist party form only a very small percentage of the total adult population. The Communists deliberately keep their party organization small, for the sake of discipline and efficiency, and because they desire to rule the masses ruthlessly through the dictatorship of a clique. Again and again, the Communists have demanded the right to carry on their activities in free nations without restraint, on the excuse that their party membership is so small as to offer no threat to established institutions. But the compact nature of Communist parties makes them the more dangerous. When the Communists seized power in Russia and China, they represented only a tiny fraction of the total population of those nations; yet they triumphed in very short order, once they had obtained control of the reins of government.

By deceit, terror, and military conquest, the Communists have seized Russia, the largest of all countries; China, the most populous of all countries; Poland, Hungary, Rumania, Bulgaria, Czechoslovakia, Yugoslavia, Albania, Latvia, Lithuania, Estonia, Tibet, and much of Germany, Korea, and Indo-China. They have temporarily obtained power, or have risen in insurrection, in several other states. They maintain cadres of agitators in nearly every other country in the world. Everywhere their tactics have been much the same, from their ferocious attempt to seize Paris and France in 1871 to their recent domination of Guatemala and their present struggle for supremacy in southeastern Asia and Indonesia. The "liquidation"—that is, the murder or imprisonment—of all their opponents or of anyone who might remotely challenge their power, from monarchists to socialists, from cardinals to shopkeepers, is their first act once they have obtained control over troops and police.

Communism inspired by hatred

The directing passion of Communism, in short, is hate. Christian compassion and Christian charity and Christian love are abhorrent to the Communist; so are the moral principles of Judaism and Islam and Buddhism and all other established religions. Appealing to the diabolical impulses in human nature, the Communists array class against class, man against man. Once triumphant, they perpetuate their clique in power by a system of police-spies and frequent purges of "deviationists" from their own ranks. Fear and suspicion torment everyone in a Communist country, from the most obscure working-people to the commissars and party leaders themselves. In the immediate backgrounds always looms up the vast concentration camp, to which are transported whoever may be accused of disloyalty toward the Communist regime, or even of lukewarmness toward Communist policy. Never in the whole history of mankind before has so large a proportion of any country's population been kept imprisoned as in the twentieth-century Communist states. Quite literally, Communist society is a living hell.

Practical results of Communist victory

As for the fulfillment of the five dogmas of theoretical Communism listed earlier in this chapter, practical Communism does indeed destroy the old order, as it promises to do; but it never succeeds in establishing the Utopia which also is promised. The practical results of Communist ascendancy are these:

(1) Although traditional religious institutions are abolished, the Communists substitute a godless religion of their own, with secular dogmas and an apparatus which is the caricature of a church. This secular religion is far less tolerant than any true religion. The pseudo-religion of Communism even canonizes "Communist saints"; the bodies of Lenin and Stalin, enshrined in Moscow, are venerated ritually. And although every effort is made to extirpate belief in God, the promised substitution of material satisfaction for the masses never achieves reality. On the contrary, the real needs of the public are neglected in favor of building military strength and carrying out grandiose state industrial projects. If one takes into consideration the general increase of productivity throughout most of the world since 1918, standards of living in Communist Russia are lower than those of Czarist Russia. Thus the consolations of religion are de-

stroyed, but the promised material satisfactions are un-
realized.

(2) Although the leadership of traditional society is
effaced by the Communists when they come to power,
the Communists never really establish equality among
men. Quite the opposite: for the Communists always
create a new elite, what has been called "a host of squalid
oligarchs," commissars and party functionaries, who rule
as absolutely as any old-fashioned aristocracy, but rule
without any moral or institutional checks upon their
power. These Communist masters justify Lord Acton's
observation that "power tends to corrupt, and absolute
power corrupts absolutely." Although the old incentives
to integrity are abolished, the Communist regime creates
the new and terrible incentives of power-lust and special
privileges for the Communist party-organizers and bureaucrats. Even the economic rewards of Communist
functionaries ordinarily are greater than the rewards of
most political and business leaders in the free nations—
especially when we take into consideration the profound
poverty of the mass of men and women in the Communist countries. So far as equality is concerned, the real
Communist belief, as George Orwell suggested in his
satire *Animal Farm,* is that "all animals are equal; but
some are more equal than others."

(3) Although Communists always—as they promise—
establish a dictatorship as soon as they achieve power,
this dictatorship is the rule of the "proletariat" or working classes only in name. In Russia, China, Poland, Hun-

gary, and everywhere else the Communists have seized power, the real "workers and peasants" whom the Communists have pretended to represent have been treated with contempt and brutality. The land promised to peasants invariably has been taken away from those peasants, so soon as the Communist regime has felt sufficiently strong, and incorporated into vast state "collective farms." The industrial workers have been crushed mercilessly whenever they attempted to protest against Communist state policies: when, in 1956, the Hungarian workingmen rose up against their Communist masters, they were shot down by tanks, shipped in thousands to Siberia, and denounced as "capitalists" and "Fascists."

(4) Although Communists continue, in power, to talk vaguely of a future period in which the Communist dictatorship itself will wither away, in plain fact the chains of servitude grow more heavy as the years pass, in every Communist state; the state becomes more and more powerful and ruthless, steadily destroying every remaining rival to its empire: churches, private property, labor unions, the family itself. "Freedom?" Lenin asked once. "What for? What for?" Since the Communist masters are hated by their subjects, they can survive only through a constant persecution of every dissenter. The state, far from withering, becomes everything.

(5) Although truly all the energies of formal education, art, literature, science, and the whole apparatus of culture are turned by the Soviets to Communist ends, this servitude of morals and learning to political ideology

results in all Communist lands in a fast and ruinous decay of the works of mind and conscience. Even some of the leading Communist "intellectuals" have ventured to protest against this destruction of culture and imagination: but only at their own great peril, and ineffectually. Communist ideology destroys high civilization.

Thus the Communists rise to total power through taking advantage of certain confusions and weaknesses in the life of the modern world. But once triumphant, the Communists do not remedy those confusions and weaknesses. On the contrary, they subject the whole of society to a terrible state of fear and insecurity—becoming more intense and general as the years pass—which frustrates the noblest longings in human nature. The Communists can destroy, but they cannot create. For love, they substitute hatred; for the uncertainties of a free society, the certain slavery of a Communist society.

Communist attacks on America

As the failure of Communist dreams and promises becomes apparent even to the Communists themselves, they seek to divert attention from their dismal caricature of Utopia by incessantly attacking, through an elaborate propaganda, the alleged failings of the free countries. They hope that people of the free world will not see the Communist beam because of the "capitalist" mote in their eyes. The United States being the present chief check upon Communist ambition, the accusations of Communist propaganda are directed with special intensity against America. Some of these Communist charges may be summarized here.

(1) America is "materialistic": civilization in the United States is oppressed by a crass concentration upon private profit.

(2) America is "imperialistic": the United States intends to dominate all the other nations of the world.

(3) America is "capitalistic": American businessmen grow rich upon the labor of the American poor.

(4) America is unjust: minorities and even majorities are repressed and bullied in the United States.

(5) America is decadent: public and private morality and culture are sinking toward utter collapse in the United States.

And there are other charges; but these five may suffice to illustrate the Communist methods in propaganda. Although nearly all Americans feel that these accusations are unfounded, too often Americans have failed to reply coherently to such charges. The Communist intention is to give Americans a bad conscience, and to give the United States a bad reputation in the rest of the world; to confuse, to obscure Communist guilt by a barrage of petty and reckless insults to the United States. The Communist propagandists are satisfied if, though failing to convince altogether, they succeed in establishing doubts about American society in men's minds; for the Communist objective is not so much to win adherents to the Communist party as simply to weaken loyalty to the United States and to dishearten America's allies.

These tactics were employed with some success in the Korean prison-camps. Our final chapter, therefore, consists in part of a brief refutation of such Communist propaganda.

CHAPTER 10

The American Answer

America is unaccustomed to world leadership. We entered both World Wars only with great reluctance, and as a nation we have not sought to profit from our victories in those conflicts. Being new to many international responsibilities, sometimes we are hesitant and overly apologetic in our policies and statements; and sometimes we blunder. Nor is our society perfect, for no society ever has been perfect, or will be. Yet ours is a just, orderly, free, prosperous, and intelligent society. By the side of Communist society, ours is a marvellous achievement. We have no need to damn ourselves with faint praise, though we ought not to fall into the opposite pit of braggadocio. Here, then, are some answers to the Communists' accusations against the United States.

America and materialism

(1) America is "materialistic" only in the sense that all men, everywhere, always have employed most of their time in getting and spending. American industry and thrift have helped to make the United States the

richest of great powers. And our material achievement renders possible a very high degree of leisure and cultural achievement among us. Honest private profit is a good thing: it produces "the wealth of nations," public prosperity.

There are many evidences that Americans are interested in much else besides getting and spending. We spend more upon formal education, per head of population, than does any other country. We have more church-goers, per capita, than has any other great state. We have an immense number of public libraries and museums of art. We have one of the highest rates of literacy in the world. The intelligence and honesty of our popular newspapers is superior to that in most countries. In our brief span of national existence, we have acquired a national literature of a distinct character and universal meaning: the work of Hawthorne, Fenimore Cooper, Melville, Holmes, Mark Twain, Henry Adams, Henry James, P. E. More, George Santayana, and many others. We have great private endowments for the advancement of culture.

Soviet materialism

And when we contrast this record with Soviet materialism, the Communist accusation becomes ludicrous. With the triumph of the Communists in Russia, Russia culture was severed as if by an axe. Literature, painting, sculpture, architecture, and even music have withered under the blight of Communist theory and practice. For the Communists, far from really disdaining "materialism," make what they call "dialectical materialism" an article of faith with all members of their party. For the thoroughgoing Communist, the only aim of life is improvement of material conditions; and the struggle for material advancement, in their theories, is the whole meaning of history. Material production, for the Soviets, is an end in itself: culture, leisure, and all the works of the mind are conscripted by the Communists to serve in the materialistic class struggle. By their obsession with material gains, the Communists have dried up the springs of creative imagination; they have even abolished the themes from which great literature is drawn.* So the Communist charge of "materialism" against the United States is not merely a case of the pot calling the kettle black: it is deliberate hypocrisy.

America and imperialism

(2) America is the least imperialistic, probably, of all great powers in all history. There is no American desire to build an empire overseas or in the Western hemisphere; nor do we attempt to secure trade monopolies abroad. We maintain garrisons in Europe and Asia to guard against the threat of Soviet conquest of our allies, but we keep those forces at a minimum, and withdraw them altogether whenever practicable. Sometimes, indeed, we may have acted with imprudence in giving up bases and positions important to our own security and that of our allies. We withdrew altogether from China after our war with Japan, for instance, even though the

* On this point, see Russell Kirk, *The Death of Art* (1955).

Communists were then engaged in overthrowing the Kuomintang government of China with which we were allied. We withdrew our troops from Korea despite Communist preparations for invading South Korea, and returned only after our small remaining forces had been attacked by the Communists. At the end of the war in Europe, we withdrew from eastern Germany, Czechoslovakia, and other territories, allowing the Communists to occupy those areas. In Indo-China, we declined to assist the French against the Communists. These are not the actions of a nation bent upon building an empire.

Our whole national history refutes the charge that Americans mean to be masters of the world. When, in 1846, we utterly defeated the Mexicans, we did not annex Mexico, though we had taken their capital. In our war with Spain, in 1898, we did not annex Cuba, where most of the war was fought. Though we acquired the Philippines, we gave those islands complete independence after we had freed them from the Japanese at the end of the Second World War. Earlier in this century, we withdrew from Central America the Marines we had sent there to restore order. We took no part in the nineteenth- and twentieth-century partition of Africa, though we certainly had the power to do so. Our only considerable outpost beyond the North American continent is Hawaii. We maintain troops in Germany and Japan only at the request of those states. This is not the way in which an imperialistic country behaves.

Nor have we been economic imperialists. Opposed to monopolies and cartels, we have stood for commercial and industrial competition throughout the world, declining to take advantage of our military strength to secure commercial agreements favorable to the United States. To many nations, we give or lend far more than we sell to them or buy from them. Since the end of the Second World War, we have given many billions of dollars to other countries without expectation of repayment. Surely no imperialistic state ever followed this policy.

Communist imperialism

Now compare these policies with those of the Soviets. Whenever Communist Russia has felt sufficiently strong, she has endeavored to enlarge her own territories at the expense of her neighbors, to force Communist regimes upon eastern Europe and Asia, and to foment Communist revolutions throughout the world. Just before the Second World War, the Communist government of Russia seized Lithuania, Latvia, and Estonia, and later deported to Siberia much of the population of those countries. Russia attacked her neighbor Finland, though she was unable to conquer that valiant little country. While China was struggling against Japan, Russia occupied Outer Mongolia. When the Second World War commenced with the German invasion of Poland, Soviet Russia seized eastern Poland, murdering thousands of Polish officers the Russians had taken prisoner. At the end of the Second World War, Soviet Russia annexed portions of Poland, Germany, Rumania, Czechoslovakia, Finland, Japan, and China. By employing Russian troops, the Soviets established unpopular Communist governments in Poland, Hungary, Rumania, Bulgaria, and later Czechoslovakia. Russia supported a puppet Communist regime in Albania, and attempted to encourage a similar regime in Greece. She created a new state, East Germany, with Communist masters. Her aid to the Chinese Communists made possible the overthrow of the Chinese government with which Russia had been allied during the Second World War. The Soviets have aided the Communists in Indo-China, Guatemala, and several other countries, and have meddled constantly in the affairs of the Arab states, particularly Syria and Egypt. They have come close, on two occasions, to establishing Communist control in part or all of Persia. And this summary does not take into account the Soviet work of subversion conducted, in varying degree, in most of the rest of the world.

Nor is this imperialism confined to Russia. Communist China has behaved similarly, seizing Tibet, sending her "volunteer" armies into Korea, and giving military assistance to the Communists of Viet Minh. No country of western Europe, even at the height of the age of European imperialism, ever behaved so ruthlessly as have these Communist imperialists, nor repressed rebellions so ferociously. The savage crushing of the Hungarians in 1956, for instance, shocked even many western European Communists. Yet Soviet propagandists continue to insist that America is an imperialist nation and that the Soviets are the champions of national freedom.

153

America and capitalism

(3) America is "capitalistic," and proudly so, in the sense that Americans believe in private property and private enterprise, and point to the fruits of that economic system. In earlier chapters of this book, we touched upon the merits of our free economy. It can stand upon its own record. It may also be emphasized that the American economy has been called a "people's capitalism," for ownership of property, including great industries, is very widely shared, and the profits go to the laborer as well as the owner and the manager. Private property is one of the chief satisfactions of life, Americans know, and private economic responsibility helps to secure public freedom.

Commissar-capitalism

By "capitalism," the Communists imply that the people who control capital are able to force the mass of men and women to work for them at wages which barely keep the working people alive. This certainly is not true in the United States, and never has been. But it is terribly true today in Soviet countries. Every civilized country has to be "capitalistic" in the sense that the existence of capital is necessary to economic production. There is capital in Russia, just as in the United States. And there are capitalists in Russia—that is, persons who control that capital. But the Communist capitalists are a much smaller class than American capitalists, and infinitely more powerful as a class. The Soviet Russian capitalists are the commissars and Communist party officials who control Soviet industry and agriculture. These Communist capitalists are supreme: there is no check upon their authority, from government or labor unions or political parties. They can, and do, force the peoples of Soviet states to work under whatever conditions they prescribe, for as small wages as they like. And those conditions often are wretched, and those wages usually are very small, because the masters of the Soviet system choose to spend most of the industrial surplus upon armaments and "Five Year Plans" and other grand state designs. There is no appeal possible from their arbitrary economic decisions.

If an American workingman is dissatisfied with the amount of his pay or the conditions of his labor, he may obtain employment elsewhere, in a free market; or he may act through his union to improve his condition. But in a Soviet system, the workingman is wholly at the disposal of his commissar-capitalist. There is only one employer, the Communist state. So far as unions exist, they are the creations of the Communist state, dominated by agents of the Communist party. And if the Soviet workingman protests against this, or fails to produce his quota, he may be sent to a slave-labor camp in the Soviet Arctic, to be worked to death like an old horse, his food-ration reduced whenever he falls below his enormous prescribed production-quota. None of the exaggerated charges of Marx and Engels against nineteenth-century capitalism accuse the private capitalists of such methods as are now employed daily by the Communist-capitalists of the Soviet states. The exploitation of the worker which Marx and his followers predicted would be carried out by the private capitalist of the future, now is executed, instead, by the disciples of Marx. It is at its worst, perhaps, in the "satellite" states, like Hungary and Czechoslovakia, where not only the workingman, but the country as a whole, is drained of its goods for the benefit of Russia. Whatever flaws there may be in the American economic system, they are indiscernible by the side of the pitiless economic servitude of the Soviets.

America and justice

(4) America is unjust only to the extent that perfect justice never has been secured anywhere, at any time in history. Justice is the securing to every man of what is his own. The civil rights and the property rights of Americans are guaranteed by federal and state constitutions, by the courts, and by centuries of usage. It is improbable that a greater measure of justice ever prevailed in any nation. There are regular means of redress for injustice: a man may appeal to the law, and to public opinion. Cases of injustice receive wide attention in America precisely because they are rare exceptions, not the rule. We take particular pains to preserve the rights of minorities; our constitutions, indeed, are intended primarily as a defense of minorities against hasty or selfish temporary majorities.

American minorities

At present, the Soviet propaganda concerning American "injustice" seizes upon the condition of the American

Negro for its chief theme. One reason for this is that there are hardly any Negroes in the Soviet Union; and therefore Americans cannot reply with a description of Communists oppression of a Negro minority. The Communists rarely say anything about the condition of the American Jews, because the Soviets have pitilessly utilized the Jews of the Soviet states for whatever might serve Soviet ends, sometimes putting them into unpopular positions of power in order to make them scapegoats, and at other times fiercely persecuting them as "bourgeois" and disloyal to Communism. At present, the policy of persecution is uppermost.

As for the American Negro, it is perfectly true that, taken as a class, Negroes are less prosperous than other Americans; and there are a number of ways in which their social condition should be improved. But that improvement is in progress, and progress has been made for many years. No other nation with so large a minority of a different color and a slave-origin has done better than has the United States in improving the lot of that minority. The American Negro has come a long way since slavery, and he will go further yet. The evils of slavery take a long while to eradicate. What is much more remarkable than the deprivations of the American Negro nowadays is the rights and opportunities which he already has obtained. The Communist propagandists make a great deal of the lynching of Negroes. But murders of Negroes by white mobs have become very rare, anywhere in the United States; there is every reason to believe that lynching will be only an ugly memory, a few years from now. Over the past decade, there have been whole years in which no such murders occurred. American justice is not decaying: it is more regularly applied with every year that passes.

Communist injustice

But in the Communist countries, the very theory of justice is denied. Justice, again, is the securing to every man of the things that belong to him. According to the Communists, no man has anything that belongs to him. Everything belongs to the proletarian dictatorship—that is, the Communist state. A man has no natural rights, and is entirely at the mercy of his dictatorial masters. Soviet courts are subject to the dictation of the Communist party; and many alleged offenses which in America would be investigated by a regular court of law, with provisions for appeal from the court's decision, in Soviet lands are decided arbitrarily by "administrative tribunals," not bound by strict legal procedures. The Soviet "purge" trials of political dissenters or "deviationists" have become infamous throughout the world for their thoroughgoing disregard of any principle of impartiality.

Communist treatment of minorities

When we turn to the Soviet conduct toward minorities, we find a triumph of mass injustice unparalleled in modern history; for even the Nazis did not persecute such enormous numbers of people as the Russians have. Soviet Russia and her satellites are ruled by a tiny minority, the Communist party elite. This arrogant minority is free to domineer over both majorities and minorities as it chooses. From 1918 to the present, the Communist leaders have engaged in deliberate persecutions without cessation; indeed, persecution seems to be necessary to the survival of the Communist regime. From time to time there have been even persecutions of elements within the Communist party. The Soviet system commenced by stamping out brutally the aristocratic and middle-class elements in Russian society—often by massacre, lynchings on a grand scale. Mass murders of this sort have been a regular instrument of the Communists ever since, wherever they have held power; they were employed, for instance, by the Communists in the Spanish Civil War, even against the other Spanish parties with whom they were leagued. Every successive development of the Soviet system has been accompanied by fresh organized persecutions: the "liquidation of the Nepmen," the small traders of the early years of the U.S.S.R.; the "expropriation of the kulaks," in which the small farmers of the Ukraine, in hundreds of thousands, were shipped off to Siberia or condemned to starvation by economic decree; the "elimination of the Old Bolsheviks," in which Stalin and his clique exterminated many of the founders of the Soviet system.

And the Soviets for many years have been stamping out systematically not simply economic and political minorities, but large religious and racial groups. Both Christian and Moslem faiths, in every part of the Soviet Union, have been subjected to treatment as severe as that meted out to the Russian Jews. The Orthodox Church has been brought under the surveillance of the Communist state, and even so is discouraged and barely tolerated at all; through the League of Militant Atheists, the Soviets have kept up an official propaganda against religion. Christianity being too widespread and deeply rooted in Russia for even a violent Soviet persecution to abolish faith overnight, the Soviets now seem to be relying principally upon anti-religious instruction in the state schools to destroy the remnants of organized Christianity.

As for racial minorities, the Communists have deliberately adopted official and long-range policies of extermination which make their hypocritical reproaches against rare and sporadic discrimination in America seem absurd. Fearing the existence of any minority as a potential center of resistance to the regime, and maintaining on principle that every man should be exactly like every other man in the Soviet world, the Communists have been eager to force out of existence the scores of Asiatic and other minority groups within their frontiers. The slave-labor camps of Siberia have become so many monstrous refuse-dumps for unwanted populations. To recite even the names and dates of all the thorough racial persecutions within the Soviets would require too much space here. It must be sufficient to mention that during and since the Second World War, the Soviets have virtually wiped out, by deportation, condemnation, and starvation, several whole peoples that had existed for thousands of years: the Crimean Tartars, the Kalmucks, the German-speaking settlements of the Volga basin, the Kuban Cossacks, the Jewish "autonomous republics," and the majority of the peoples of Latvia and Estonia. And, having done all this without a tear, the masters of the Soviet system shake their heads mournfully at the alleged failures of "capitalist" justice in the United States and the rest of the free world.

America and decadence

(5) Decadence, according to C. E. M. Joad, is "the loss of an object." A man is decadent who has ceased to have any aim in life; a society is decadent that no longer perceives goals and standards. Measured by this test, the United States remains a vigorous and hopeful society. Most Americans recognize objects in life. To do their duty under God; to rear decent families; to improve their own condition, and that of their community; to educate themselves; to acquire a home and other property; to maintain the best in their civilization—these goals continue to attract many millions of Americans. Foreign observers are impressed generally with the vigor and strength of fiber in American character. One of these, a Scot, Mr. J. M. Reid, remarks that "freedom, simplicity, and diversity" still are the marks of American civilization. And he continues:

Thinking Americans are worried about many of the things that disturb us too—about the future of a civilization which seems, increasingly, to base its life and hopes on inessential gadgets, about the complications of industrialization, and technology, and the hideous threat to life itself that these things have developed, about the weakening, or absence, of traditional leadership and generally accepted standards of culture. The very form that these worries take, however, is striking and even hopeful to a European. You still feel, as we once did, that the individual should be able to do something effective about the things that trouble him, whereas most of us have come to think that what is wrong with our world is beyond our control—that our best hope is to escape disaster for ourselves, not to prevent it for the people and places we know. We feel ourselves to be already half-defeated, whereas your world still seems a manageable one, though it may be difficult to handle.*

No, America is not the nation of Kinsey Report subjects, inane television-viewers, and Hollywood addicts that Communist propaganda describes. The inventiveness, the industry, and the confidence in the goodness of life which are the symptoms of private and social health remain vigorous among us. Americans are willing to point out their own society's shortcomings, which is another indication that decadence is not upon us. A decadent man and a decadent people ordinarily confess to no faults, because they have lost sight of the standards by which virtue and vice are determined.

Decadence of Communist system

But what of the Communists? Is it possible that the Communists are the modern decadents? Decadence is the loss of an object. What objects in existence do Communists recognize? They do not have for an aim the love

* J. M. Reid, "Three Words on America," *Modern Age,* Summer, 1957.

of God, for they have denied God's existence. They do not indulge the hope of immortality, for they have denounced the idea of immortality as a bourgois sham. They do not hold out the end of love of mankind, for they preach class hatred and warfare. They cannot seek the betterment of family, for under Communism family is swallowed up by the proletarian state, and special regard for kindred is close to treason. They must not try to improve their own condition, for that would be to establish inequality. They find themselves unable to improve the local community, for central direction resents local autonomy, and true community has been engulfed by that Leviathan proletarian dictatorship. Their Communist education is no satisfaction, for it is intended only to turn out obedient state servants and efficient technicians, not truly human persons. As for their homes, they are mere temporary nests, and cannot be passed on to their posterity, or be made to reflect the personality of their occupants. They cannot struggle to preserve the best in civilization, the "ashes of their fathers and the temples of their gods," because Communist doctrine denounces and abhors the legacy of the past. When these objects have been excluded—or, as the Communists would say in their grim jargon, "have been liquidated"— very little remains that makes life worth living.

The hopes of Communists must be confined to a narrow compass. They may aspire to make the Communist party ever stronger and more ruthless. They may hope to rivet the fetters of Communism ever more closely upon the captive nations. They may strive to drive out of the world all love, all poetry, all variety, all private integrity, all ancient loyalties, all moral standards, and even the awareness of God. They are still permitted, in short, to have one object in life: and that object is hatred. They are not permitted to build, but they are ordered to destroy. The heart and the mind wither under such constriction of ends and aims. A man who has exchanged love for hate, principle for fanaticism, art for propaganda, philosophy for slogans, aspiration for envy, imagination for dreary secular dogmas—there is the true decadent of modern times. The architects of this genuine decadence were Marx and Lenin and Stalin. They deprived one-third of mankind of an object in life.

American promise

To save the rest of the world from this decadence, this collectivistic life-in-death, is a part of the American cause. "Observe good faith and justice toward all nations," President Washington said in his Farewell Address, more than a hundred and sixty years ago, to his fellow Americans. "Cultivate peace and harmony with all. Religion and morality enjoin this conduct; and can it be that good policy does not equally enjoin it? It will be worthy of a free, enlightened, and at no distant period, a great nation, to give to mankind the magnanimous and too novel example of a people always guided by an exalted justice and benevolence."

America now is a great nation; and if she is not invariably guided by an exalted justice and benevolence, still surely she is playing her part among the nations

with some courage and generosity. For two important
reasons—and those of equal weight in the minds of most
citizens of the United States—America has set her face
against Communism and the other totalist ideologies,
stationed her troops on foreign soil, built an immense
air-force and an immense fleet, poured out her national
wealth in aid of the defence and the welfare of the free
world. One reason is that Americans believe in the dignity of man, made in an image more than human; and the
Communists threaten to destroy that dignity wherever
they find weakness. The other reason is that Americans
know they themselves cannot be secure unless the civilization of which they are a part is secure. They have not
hesitated to oppose by strength the armed doctrine of
Communism. Their cause, they feel, is the cause of true
human nature, of enlightened order, regular justice, and
liberty under law.

Americans do not aspire to make the world into one
vast uniform United States; for they cherish diversity at
home and abroad. Their present high hope is simply that,
God willing, they may keep the world from being crushed
into the iron mold of Soviet collectivism. For this cause
they have made some sacrifices; they will make more.
That our elaborate civilization and our delicate civil
social order may not fall victims to the decadence called
Communism: this is the end to which American policy
is directed nowadays. And if Americans have valor in
them still, theirs will not be a losing cause.

SUGGESTED READINGS

Suggested Readings

The books and documents listed below are merely a few of the many which might well be suggested. This very short bibliography is intended simply to name some works of especial interest concerned with American history, politics, economics, and religious opinion, and also some studies of Communism and Communist indoctrination.

BOOKS AND PAMPHLETS

Boorstin, Daniel J. *The Genius of American Politics.* Chicago: University of Chicago Press, 1953.

Brownson, Orestes. *Selected Essays.* Edited by Russell Kirk. Chicago: Gateway Editions, 1955.

Budenz, Louis. *The Techniques of Communism.* Chicago: Henry Regnery, 1954.

Burnham, James. *The Web of Subversion.* Philadelphia: John Day, 1954.

Chambers, Whittaker. *Witness.* New York: Random House, 1952.

Chamberlin, William Henry. *Beyond Containment.* Chicago: Henry Regnery, 1953.

Eliot, T. S. *The Idea of a Christian Society.* New York: Harcourt, Brace, 1939.

Gentz, Friedrich. *The French and American Revolutions Compared.* Edited by Russell Kirk. Chicago: Gateway Editions, 1955.

Gray, Alexander. *The Socialist Tradition: Moses to Lenin.* New York: Longmans, Green, 1946.

Hallowell, John H. *The Moral Foundation of Democracy*. Chicago: University of Chicago Press, 1954.

Hayek, Friedrich A. *The Road to Serfdom*. Chicago: University of Chicago Press, 1940.

Hoffman, Ross J. S. *The Spirit of Politics and the Future of Freedom*. Milwaukee: Bruce, 1951.

Hunter, Edward. *Brain-Washing in Red China*. New York: Vanguard, 1951.

Hunter, Edward. *Brainwashing: the Story of the Men who Defied It*. New York: Farrar, Strauss, 1956.

Kennedy, Malcolm D. *A History of Communism in East Asia*. New York: Praeger, 1957.

Kirk, Russell. *The Conservative Mind*. Chicago: Henry Regnery, 1953.

Kirk, Russell. *The Death of Art* (published in the same volume with Ilya Ehrenburg's *The Thaw*). Chicago: Henry Regnery, 1955.

Kirk, Russell. *Randolph of Roanoke*. Chicago: University of Chicago Press, 1951.

Lippmann, Walter. *The Public Philosophy*. Boston: Little, Brown, 1954.

Lowry, Charles Wesley. *Communism and Christ*. New York: Morehouse–Gorham, 1952.

Lukacs, John A. *The Great Powers and Eastern Europe*. Chicago: Henry Regnery, 1954.

Marx, Karl. *Capital*. Various editions.

Marx, Karl, and Engels, Friedrich. *The Communist Manifesto*. Introduction by Stefan Possony. Chicago: Gateway Editions, 1954.

McGovern, William M., and Collier, David S. *Radicals and Conservatives*. Chicago: Henry Regnery, 1957.

Meerloo, Joost A. M. *The Rape of the Mind: the Psychology of Thought Control, Menticide, and Brainwashing*. Cleveland: World, 1956.

Nef, John U. *The United States and Civilization*. Chicago: University of Chicago Press, 1948.

Suggested Readings

Niemeyer, Gerhart, with the assistance of Reshetar, John S., Jr *An Inquiry into Soviet Mentality*. New York: Praeger, 1956.

Orton, William A. *The Economic Role of the State*. Chicago: University of Chicago Press, 1950.

Pate, Lloyd W. *Reactionary!* As told to B. J. Cutler. New York: Harper, 1956.

Rauch, Georg von. *A History of Soviet Russia*. New York: Praeger, 1957.

Rigney, Harold W., S.V.D. *Four Years in a Red Hell*. Chicago: Henry Regnery, 1956.

Röpke, Wilhelm. *The Social Crisis of Our Time*. Chicago: University of Chicago Press, 1950.

Rossiter, Clinton. *Seedtime of the Republic: the Origin of the American Tradition of Political Liberty*. New York: Harcourt, Brace, 1953.

Strauss, Leo. *Natural Right and History*. Chicago: University of Chicago Press, 1953.

Thorin, Duane. *A Ride to Panmunjom*. Chicago: Henry Regnery, 1956.

Tocqueville, Alexis de. *Democracy in America*. Various editions.

Voegelin, Eric. *The New Science of Politics*. Chicago: University of Chicago Press, 1952.

Weaver, Richard M. *Ideas Have Consequences*. Chicago: University of Chicago Press, 1948.

Wilson, Francis Graham. *The American Political Mind*. New York: McGraw-Hill, 1947.

Wright, David McCord. *Democracy and Progress*. New York: Macmillan, 1946.

GOVERNMENT DOCUMENTS

Communist Interrogation, Indoctrination and Exploitation of American Military and Civilian Prisoners. Report of the Committee on Government Operations made by its Perma-

171

nent Subcommittee on Investigations. 84th Congress, 2d Session, Senate Report No. 2832. Washington: United States Government Printing Office, 1957.

Communist Interrogation, Indoctrination, and Exploitation of Prisoners of War. Department of the Army Pamphlet No. 30-101. Washington: Department of the Army, May, 1956.